The Concept of
Corporate Strategy

The Concept of Corporate Strategy

Kenneth R. Andrews

Donald Kirk David Professor of
Business Administration Emeritus
Harvard University
Third Edition

1987

Homewood, Illinois 60430

ISBN 0-256-03629-2

Library of Congress Catalog Card No. 86–81803

Printed in the United States of America

5 6 7 8 9 0 ML 4 3 2 1 0 9

Preface

This book, originally published in 1971, revised in 1980, and presented now in a third edition, is still dedicated to this classically simple idea: The highest function of an executive is leading the continuous process that shapes the nature of an organization and determines, revises, and achieves its purposes. Management in the business enterprise is the art form I have in mind. But educational institutions, other nonprofit undertakings, governments, and associations of professionals have as much or greater need for the kind of strategic management described here. The central idea applies equally to individuals who, rather than drift through life, wish to contribute to the purposes of organizations and society that are worth serving.

The substance of this book is essentially that of another titled *Business Policy: Text and Cases,* also published by Richard D. Irwin, Inc. This casebook in business policy, widely used in business schools and executive education programs, currently appears in its sixth edition, with C. Roland Christensen, Joseph L. Bower, Michael E. Porter, Richard G. Hamermesh, and me as its compilers. This version of the current text is published for use by the executive readers who will apply it in detail to their own companies as their single crucial case. It is available also to educators to use with sequences of cases different from the selection we offer. The hundreds of case studies undertaken over the years to understand how policy decisions are made in business have made possible a practitioner-oriented theory of general management. Company cases disciplined by field research skills and standards reveal, when subjected to the analytical approach described here, how the process of decision making might become more accurate and productive.

That strategic decision should be more accurate and productive has become obvious. During the decade of the 1980s American business management, taken as a whole, faltered in world competition. The emulative Japanese, in particular, are popularly thought to have surpassed American managers in techniques for increasing productivity, speeding up the transition of new products from laboratory to market, and winning consumer loyalty with reliable high quality. They are held to be equally skilled in cooperating with government to succeed in export markets rather than only competing with each other domestically. The rise of Japanese industry has been blessed by temporary advantages like the strength of the dollar in relation to the yen and supported by ingenious forms of protectionism. But its real accomplishment cannot be denied.

As we have become used to seeing Japanese industry progress from low-cost production of standard products to world-class performance in high technology products like electronics and ceramics, it has become evident that the crucial difference between American and Japanese management is strategic perspective. In the United States, the pressure to keep quarterly earnings increasing regularly to support share price is intense. Huge pension funds are managed by persons judged by short-term performance who have the legal fiduciary obligation and vulnerability to lawsuit which encourages them to maximize real short-term benefits to the disadvantage of intangible and uncertain future benefits. Financial institutions are similarly pressed to trade large blocks of shares on news of immediate rather than long-term import. Capital for corporate development costs much more in the United States than in Japan.

As is well known the pressures for steadily improving quarter-by-quarter earnings is moderated in Japan by bank ownership of company shares, the recognition that modernization of plant, development of new technology and products, and movement into world markets take time, and reward systems that do not depend on executive virtuosity. In a combination of circumstance, vulnerability, loyalty to the value of hard work, product quality, and modest as well as further reaching innovation, Japanese management appears to be more truly strategic than improvisatory.

The interesting difference between American and Japanese strategic management lies in the time dimension. The years required for individual firms to transform themselves from producers of cheap goods of low quality to companies commanding world respect became available because of the consent and patience of the providers of capital, the owners of companies, the managers and other employees. A national consensus was struck to assert that in the absence of natural resources survival meant allegiance to the long-term goal of equaling or surpassing world standards of performance in the conversion of raw materials and technologies into finished product. The concentration of capital and labor on goals approved by the government, the single-minded convergence of individual effort on company objectives, and the fervent support by a homogeneous society of a national strategy have resulted in a spectacular application of determination. The resources at hand, the distinctive capability of an industrious people, the values they hold and their sense of responsibility to their companies and their companies' responsibility to their society, and the commitment that animates the pursuit of purpose combine in an almost too-perfect and larger-than-life illustration of the concept of corporate strategy.

Imitation of Japan as such, however, will never be on the American agenda. Ethnic and cultural variety, confrontational disorder in the relations between government and business, and the values attached to individualism would make direct emulation impossible, even if desired. But establishing and defending concern for the more distant rather than the immediate future need not be a subordinate characteristic of the American business system.

The strong pressures for achieving short-term results at the expense of investment in the future need not always be given into. The interests of financial institutions and managers of pension funds do reach into the corporation to impose financial constraints and to displace long-term development of products and markets. But mature corporate executives are aware that balancing short-term and long-term performance is the central challenge of professional management. Substantial corporations have long since turned away from equity offerings to financing growth through retained earnings and long-term debt. Large investments do continue to be made in research and product development. In fact, of the almost $100 billion expended in 1984 for research and development, three-quarters of that amount was invested by companies rather than by government. Large amounts of venture capital are available to start-up companies as entrepreneurship promises to be more lucrative than investment in lackluster large companies in mature industries. The growth of research and development limited partnerships suggests that capital is available for future development.

But because the trade-offs between short-term returns and investment in future returns cannot be precisely calculated, the short term prevails whenever the defenses of long-term purposes are weak. The uncertainty of future returns biases discounted cash flow analysis toward the near future. Most limited R&D partnerships favor companies whose products promise to come to the market in three years. Quantification of near-at-hand results always seems surer than distant possibilities. The argument of this book is that pressure-induced distortions of the appropriate balance can be countered. Management of a corporation with a future better than its past requires clarification of company objectives, confidence that comes from commitment to a future-oriented program of action, and determination that careful formulation of plans rationally supports.

The concept of corporate strategy, originated in the United States, has been widely explored, extensively developed, and even subscribed to by much of the management community. The number of consulting firms, business schools, and practitioners who believe they subscribe to strategic management and educate others in its mysteries are legion. We will look later at why the concept has not brought the whole of American business to terms with the strategy-destroying short-term pressures that often dominate management decision. These pressures persist for stubborn reasons we will examine.

In the meantime we should note that the idea of corporate strategy emerged from the study of what has been called business policy—now often designated strategic management—in the professional schools of management.

Business policy is the study of the functions and responsibilities of the senior management in a company, the crucial problems that affect the success of the total enterprise, and the decisions that determine its direction, shape its future, and produce the results desired. The policy problems of business, like those of policy in public affairs, have to do with the choice of purposes, the development and recognition of organization identity and character, the unending definition of what needs to be done, the mobilization of resources for the attainment of goals in the face of aggressive competition or adverse circumstance, and the definitions of standards for the enforcement of responsible and ethical behavior.

The concept of strategy has developed during the past 20 years out of a long effort to perfect an integrative capstone course in the MBA curriculum—one devoted to the problems of the company *as a whole* as seen from the perspective of the president or chief executive. Its format has traditionally included complex cases, continually renewed, that present as far as practicable the total situation of a company. Students are asked to analyze the position of the company, to identify the principal problems in its situation, and to prescribe a program of action. They soon discover that only the determination of suitable objectives makes possible a satisfactorily rational choice among action alternatives. The discussion of individual companies matures into a consideration of how to formulate an appropriate pattern of purpose and policy and how to convert plans into results. How to get results is harder to teach and to learn in a classroom than on the scene. This difficulty may explain the neglect in business education of the art of implementation in favor of the analysis of potentially ideal strategies.

The business policy course, required of MBA students for decades—at Harvard and at many other universities—has in many variations often comprised the core course of university and company executive programs. At Harvard in particular, where the MBA program is directed to the practice of management rather than to the mastery of one or more related academic disciplines, courses in marketing, production, and control, for example, culminate often in consideration of strategic issues.

The knowledge, skills, and attitudes developed in such study comprise the professional orientation of the generalist who can apply analytical intelligence, entrepreneurial imagination, and administrative ability to opportunity.

Through the influence of MBA graduates, especially those entering consulting firms newly established or diversified to conduct a practice in strategic planning, the long-standing natural resistance of freewheeling improvisers, softened in executive seminars, has apparently been worn down. The path from education to practice can be followed, for example, in the General Electric Company, where since 1964 an intensive course in general management has been offered at its Crotonville institute to the many potential general managers developed in the course of the company's operations and other development programs. When strategic planning was introduced into General Electric, beginning in 1970, the strategic business unit (SBU), a combination of operations united by fundamental and long-range interconnections, ultimately became important in GE's management structure and processes. A series of workshops for strategic planners was devised to prepare staff for the SBUs and to extend in procedural and substantive detail the earlier course in the formulation and evolution of corporate strategy. A thorough preparation for what is now often called *strategic management* has resulted in acceptance of the importance of making current decisions in the context of long-range plans.

The courses were designed and taught by professional educators. The organization structure and planning processes emerged from the work of a major consulting firm. The convergence of management education and consulting practice became acceptable because of the appearance of a concept of strategy that was recognized by experienced general managers as effective and powerful in practice.

In the General Electric Company, as in many other large organizations, strategy became largely a staff function. The uncertainty of the future growth of markets, the environmental development bound to affect the hundreds of diverse businesses in which GE engaged, and the alternatives for investment and acquisition inviting investigation led to the development of a large strategic planning staff department that made recommendations for consideration by managers under pressure to make budgeted quarterly goals.

Ultimately, with a change in top management and a general disenchantment with formal strategic planning, GE's central staff was sharply reduced and strategic decision returned to division managers charged with the task of making their units the first or second performers in their industries or face divestiture. The simple stringency of this directive returns the task of achieving such a goal to the division manager. The implication is that demands for investment and long-term development of superiority require immediate attention. The need to combine short-term achievement with long-term maintenance of a leading position has led to a definition of what are the core as opposed to the peripheral businesses in this one exemplary company and establishment of clearer criteria for making long-range investments. As we will see later, the quality of performance and successful experience over time in competition are crucial determinants of the direction in which a business should be pointed.

Meanwhile, similar developments elsewhere made *strategy* a favorite word, however unclear its meaning. The apparent triumph of the concept had still a hollow sound, for the machinery of long-range planning sometimes obscured critical choices, smothered innovation in financial analysis and hesitation, and produced line resistance to staff technocrats. When oversimplified in careless hands, portfolio analysis, for example, in which the various businesses of a multiproduct company are analyzed separately for their future prospects, leads more directly to classification and ranking of businesses than to determining their place, if any, in a unified company strategy. Growth and market-share goals and arbitrarily chosen financial objectives are sometimes mistaken for a considered statement of corporate purpose. Thoughtless use of the term has resulted in purposeless motion and distracting noise.

As its meaning has dispersed throughout recent usage, the word *strategy* still retains a close connection to a conscious purpose and implies a time dimension reaching into the future. At its simplest, a strategy can be a very specific plan of action directed at a specified result within a specified period of time. A sales force may develop a plan, for example, to take away an account from a competitor, in which the goal is to get its business by July 1987. What it plans to do is in this limited context a strategy; if a company is strategically managed it will be related at once to more comprehensive forms of marketing strategy like pricing. At any rate, *functional strategy* (for example, in marketing, manufacturing, research and development, and finance) can be identified in any consciously managed company—it is the combination of purpose and policies that guides the conduct of the function. A marketing strategy in the company we just cited may be in part to lease its machinery in preference to selling it outright, but its financial strategy becomes of crucial importance in that case. The goal of functional strategy is recognizable as natural to the function, like market share for marketing, efficiency for manufacturing, and return on investment for finance. But once again the interrelation of functional strategies determines their validity.

The term *business strategy* usually refers to the product-market choices made by division or product-line management in a diversified company. It comprises the combination of relevant functional strategies. The choice is presumably made after examining the behavior of competitors, the risks and opportunities in the market, the resources that can be coaxed out of the company, and the proven strength of the division. It is usually expressed in economic and competitive terms primarily and presupposes no discontinuity in the prospects or characteristics of the product concerned. Its time span is relatively short.

The concept of *corporate strategy,* which is defined in Chapter 2, is comprehensive enough to include the business strategies guiding the divisions or product lines of a diversified company. Like business strategy, it includes both formulation and implementation, which interact upon each other. Like business strategy, it defines products and markets—and determines the company's course into the almost indefinite future. Sooner or later corporate strategy incorporates nonfinancial goals in organization, human, and ethical terms. A company will have only one corporate strategy but may incorporate into its concept of itself several business strategies.

This progression in the kinds of strategy recalls the accordion word *policy,* which can determine payment for overtime at one extreme or position a firm in its markets at the other. As we ascend from a specific strategy to corporate strategy, we pass from specific economic objectives to broader organization goals. More weight is given to such characteristics as unity, coherence, consistency, purpose, and concern for the future. The time horizon grows more distant and market-share percentages give way to a more comprehensive vision of the company's development as an institution.

Although many variations in the use of a strategic vocabulary can be detected in any conversation in business or academic life, *strategic management* is becoming recognized as the administration of operations dominated by purpose and by consideration of future opportunity, with explicit attention given to the need to clarify or change strategy as results suggest and to enter the future on a predetermined course. Its most abstract form would be the supervision of the process within complex organizations through which strategy is formulated and monitored. *Strategic planning,* if used with *strategic management,* usually refers to the staff apparatus of long-range planning. Support activities like market research, evaluation of strategic alternatives, market performance and portfolio analysis, competitive intelligence, and environmental surveillance can fall within this activity. It can also be used to refer to all preparation for the future and as a synonym for the formulation (but not the achievement) of corporate strategy.

As this book will make clear, none of the modern paraphernalia of strategic planning need deter anyone from considering a simple practitioner's theory that begins in the determination of corporate purpose in economic, human, and social terms. The idea of corporate strategy brings all the special functions of business to bear on the principal task of the chief executive. It is capable of including the most extensive combination of interrelated variables involved in the most important of all business decisions.

This idea cannot be brought to final fruition in this book or any other. It is only in an industry, company, and specific situation that its power can be realized. As you experiment with its application to your own responsibilities you will encounter its advantages.

Clarification of the character and purposes of a company and establishing the linkage of character and purpose to all its operations have many uses. An articulate corporate strategy permits every company to distinguish itself from its competitors and establish a competitive advantage. It can keep the technical knowledge of the specialist focused on the primary purpose of the corporation rather than on the parochial concerns of technical functions. It requires conscious attention to the future equal in emphasis to the superficially more urgent demands of the present. It calls for the deliberate balancing of short-term and long-term considerations, which, as I have said, are usually in conflict. It exercises the mind and teases it out of complacence with success. It makes at least partially explicit the intuitive inclinations, judgments, and values that underlie business decisions and allows the inconsistency among them and their untested validity to be examined.

During the past two decades the idea that a company's future may be less perilous if its resources and market opportunities are consciously linked in a choice that defines its business and distinguishes it from competitors has been widely discussed and often practiced. That development of a concept of corporate strategy still has not replaced improvisation as a mode of management means only that acumen, organizational skill, and determination are required to make it work. Its powers are real but not magical.

To be uncertain of the course to follow en route to an unknowable future is human. To waver from a course because of unfavorable and unexpected events is normal. To fend off the judgments of shareholders who feel no obligations of ownership is as hard as to convince financial analysts that two years of flat earnings must be invested in the next generation of products. The distractions of hostile tender offers are more urgent than long-term planning; they are all-absorbing. The attraction of large executive compensation means that performance measurable now seems more important than awaiting the future impact of present investment.

How a strategy can be devised that circumvents such facts of life is the subject of this book. It is possible to contain the counter-strategic distortions of capital markets, the provincialism of functional specialists, and the impediments posed by law and government action to constrain competition in the world marketplace. It is not only possible but also essential to plot a course into a future that cannot be foretold and to develop organization strengths that can keep a company adaptive and make it innovative.

But how to do this cannot be expressed in a formula or set of slogans. Pursuing excellence becomes possible only when we know and decide excellence in what and the criteria by which it is recognized. Being "close to the customer" is naturally desirable, but with respect to what and to what needs the customer has not recognized?

That there are no ready answers to persistent problems is well known. The susceptibility of the business community to successive brands of oversimplification and limited-purpose techniques is the triumph of need over common sense. The approach offered here is a realistic way of thinking about organization and purpose. Its outcome must be unique to the capabilities of your company, the development in your industry, and the values you and your associates hold. I cannot know the possibilities in your situation. But you can. I expect this tested description of a simple practitioner-oriented conceptual framework to prove productive. If it does, the strategy that emerges will be of your making. Its quality will reflect yours.

The chapters that follow deal first with the formulation of corporate strategy and later with its implementation. As you read them, undertake a strategic analysis of your own organization or of that presented to you in a business policy case. You should attempt a statement of what the purposes of your company are, as deduced from what it does and how it works. To determine their validity you will attempt to examine the economic environment of the company, to determine the essential characteristics of its industry, to notice developments and trends affecting future opportunity and risk. To do this, you may need to get information and to raise questions of others. You will need to appraise the strengths and weaknesses of the company when it is viewed against the background of its competition and environment. You will want to estimate its capacity to *alter* as well as to *adapt* to the forces affecting it. Strategic analysis then requires a tentative decision putting market opportunity and corporate capability together into a suitably entrepreneurial combination. It is a mind-stretching exercise.

As you think about this decision you will encounter many feasible alternatives. Your own preferences for the kind of product and the level of quality for price to be offered the consumer will influence your choice of products and market and make it different from your associates'. Your values will influence your judgment. The values of your associates will condition their reaction to your recommendations and decisions.

At some point you will realize the full measure of the new skill required. The strategic decision is the one that helps determine the nature of the business in which a company is to engage and the kind of company it is to be. It is effective for a long time. It has wide ramifications. It is the most important kind of decision to be made for the company. It requires the best judgment and analysis that can be brought to it.

But analysis is not the whole of the task implied by the concept of strategy. Once the entrepreneurial decision has been identified, the resources of the organization must be mobilized to make it effective. Achieving the commitment of the organization to the future implied by a strategy is as important as the quality of design.

To see how the complexity of choice among all the possibilities confronting a person or a company can be understood and managed by application of the idea of corporate strategy is an exciting illumination. Such insight banishes irresolution, empowers leadership, and unleashes the suppressed capability of organizations.

Contents

Chapter 1
Chief Executive Officer, President, or General Manager:
Roles and Responsibilities   1
What General Management Is. Complexity of General
Management Tasks. Chief Executive as Organization Leader.
Chief Executive as Personal Leader. Chief Executive as
Architect of Purpose. Enormity of the Task. Need for a Concept.

Chapter 2
The Concept of Corporate Strategy   13
What Strategy Is. Summary Statements of Strategy. Reasons
for Not Articulating Strategy. Deducing Strategy from
Behavior. Formulation of Strategy. The Implementation of
Strategy. Kinds of Strategies: *Low-Growth Strategies. Forced-
Growth Strategies.* Kinds of Companies. Criteria for Evaluation.
Problems in Evaluation.

Chapter 3
The Company and Its Environment: Relating
Opportunities to Resources   35
The Nature of the Company's Environment. Tracking the
Changing Environment. Identification of Opportunities and
Risks. Opportunity as a Determinant of Strategy. Identifying
Corporate Competence and Resources. Application to Situations.

Chapter 4
The Company and Its Strategists: Relating Corporate
Strategy to Personal Values   53
Strategy as Projection of Preference. The Inevitability of Values.
Reconciling Divergent Values. Modification of Values.
Awareness of Values.

Chapter 5
The Company and Its Responsibilities to Society:
Relating Corporate Strategy to Ethical Values   **65**
  Public Opinion of Managerial Malfeasance. The Inherently
  Amoral Corporation. The Moral Component of Corporate
  Strategy. The Social Responsibility of Business. Categories of
  Concern: *Review of Management Concerns for Responsibility.*
  Impact of Control Systems on Ethical Performance. The
  Individual and the Corporation. The Range of Concerns. Choice
  of Strategic Alternatives for Social Action. Determination of
  Strategy.

Chapter 6
The Implementation of Strategy: Achieving Commitment
to Purpose   **81**
  Distorted Approaches to Implementation. Flexibility in Pursuit
  of Purpose. Implementation in the Innovative Corporation.
  Structure, Coordination, and Information Systems.
  Commitment. Strategy as the Key to Simplicity.

Chapter 7
The Implementation of Strategy: From Commitment
to Results   **97**
  Establishment of Standards and Measurement of Performance.
  Fallacy of the Single Criterion. Need for Multiple Criteria.
  Effective Evaluation of Performance. Motivation and Incentives:
  Executive Compensation. Role of Incentive Pay. Nonmonetary
  Incentives. Constraints and Control: *Formal Control. Integrating*
  Formal and Social Control. Enforcing Ethical Standards.
  Recruitment and Development of Management: *Continuing*
  Education. Management Development and Corporate Purpose.

Chapter 8
Strategic Management and Corporate Governance   **113**
  Strategy as a Process. Managing the Process. The Strategic
  Function of the Board of Directors.

Index   **129**

Chapter 1

Chief Executive Officer, President, or General Manager: Roles and Responsibilities

What General Management Is

Business policy is essentially the study of the knowledge, skills, and attitudes constituting general management. Management itself may be defined as leadership in the informed, efficient, planned, and purposeful conduct of complex organized activity. General management is, in its simplest form, the management of a total enterprise or of an autonomous subunit. Its diverse forms in all kinds of businesses always include the integration of the work of functional managers or specialists.

The senior *general* manager in any organization is its chief executive officer; he or she may be called chairman of the board, president, or managing director. The title *general manager* may designate a less senior divisional or departmental post, but as a term may be used to designate all members of the hierarchy of general management—members of the office of the president, executive and senior vice presidents who have interfunctional responsibilities, and presidents or managers of divisions, multifunctional profit centers, and similar partially autonomous organization units. The point of view of general management, though not its full practice, is also essential to others—to outside directors, financial analysts, consultants, for example, who cannot accurately evaluate general management without knowing what it is. A total organization perspective is also important to senior functional officers whose concern is more for the contribution their subspecialists make to the operating organization than for the technical complexity of their work.

In this chapter we will examine the complexity of the general manager's job and the roles, functions, and skills that it requires. We are in quest of a point of view and organizing perspective that reduces to practicable order the otherwise impossible agenda of the chief executive of any organization—large or small.

The position of the chief executive is the best vantage point from which to view the processes involved in (1) the conception of organization purpose, (2) the commitment of an organization to evolving but deliberately chosen purposes, and (3) the integrated effort appropriate to achieving purpose and sustaining adaptability.

Complexity of General Management Tasks

General managers face such an array of functions and must exercise so varied a set of skills that they must acquire a formidable versatility. If you were to see a successful entrepreneur invent and perfect a proprietary product, set up a company, devise a merchandising and distribution program of a very special kind suited to protect the product against substitutes, decide to maintain year-round production in a cyclical industry to meet the needs of a highly skilled work force, establish a research and development unit to make product diversification possible, set up methods of financing high inventory and rapid growth, recruit and put in place functional managers, and later choose a successor and withdraw from supervision of the company, you would necessarily conclude that such a general manager must be successful in a variety of roles.

Consider the less varied case of a professionally trained MBA who moves up a functional hierarchy to become general manager of a division of the same organization 20 years after its founding. This person finds that the roles he or she plays and the responsibilities to be exercised within the roles differ according to the problem identified or the decision pending, the needs of the organization, or the needs and style of the CEO. In either case the simple-minded adherence to one role—a personality-determined one, for example—will leave general managers miscast much of the time as the human drama they preside over unfolds.

We are in great need of a simple way to comprehend the total responsibility of chief executives. To multiply the list of tasks they must perform and the personal qualities they would do well to have would put general management capability beyond that of reasonably well-endowed human beings. Corporate presidents are accountable for everything that goes on in their organizations. They must preside over a total enterprise made up often of technical specialties in which they cannot possibly have personal expertise. They must know their company's markets and the ways in which they are changing. They must lead private lives as citizens in their communities and as family members, as individuals with their own needs and aspirations. Except for rare earlier experience, perhaps as general managers of profit centers in their own organizations, they have found no opportunity to practice being president before undertaking the office. New presidents are obliged to put behind them the specialized apparatus their education and functional experience have provided. Engineers, for example, who continue to run their companies strictly as engineers will soon encounter financial and marketing problems, among others, that may force their removal as president.

Many attempts to characterize executive roles and functions come to very little, especially when they attempt to categorize in detail an almost infinite variety. The simplification that may best serve our approach to general management is to view its activities as assignable to three roles—*organization leader, personal leader, and architect of organization purpose.* As organization leader or manager of persons grouped in a hierarchy of suborganizations, the general manager can be called taskmaster, mediator, motivator, or organization designer, but theoretical distinctions among such illustrative categories become fruitless. The personal influence of leaders becomes evident as they play such roles as communicator, exemplar, or focus for respect or affection. The chief executive's role as architect of organization purpose is the principal subject of this book. This simple three-part separation of roles will enable us to identify the critical responsibilities and skills appropriate to each category. It is the reader's experience that will give these categories meaning and prepare the way for a new or more disciplined concept of management.

Chief Executive as Organization Leader

Chief executives, presidents, chief operating officers, and general managers are first and probably least pleasantly persons who are responsible for results attained in the present as designated by plans made previously. Nothing that we will say about their concern for the people in their organizations or about their responsibility to society can gainsay this immediate truth. Achieving acceptable results against expectations of increased earnings per share and return on the stockholder's investment requires the CEO or president to be continually informed and ready to intervene when results fall below what had been expected. Changing circumstances and competition produce emergencies upsetting well-laid plans. Resourcefulness in responding to crisis is a skill most successful executives develop early.

But the organizational consequences of the critical taskmaster role require executives to go beyond insistence upon achievement of planned results. They must see as their second principal function the creative maintenance and development of the organized capability that makes achievement possible. This activity leads to a third principle—the integration of the specialist functions that enable their organizations to perform the technical tasks in marketing, research and development, manufacturing, finance, control, and personnel that proliferate as technology develops and tend to lead the company in all directions. If this coordination is successful in harmonizing special staff activities, general managers will probably have gotten organizations to accept and order priorities in accordance with the companies' objectives. Securing commitment to purpose is a central function of the president as organization leader.

The skills required by these functions reveal presidents not solely as taskmasters, but as mediators and motivators as well. They need ability in the education and motivation of people and the evaluation of their performance, two functions that tend to work against one another. The former requires understanding of individual needs, which persist no matter what the economic purpose of the organization may be. The latter requires objective assessment of the technical requirements of the task assigned. The capability required here is also that required in the integration of functions and the mediation of the conflict bound to arise out of technical specialism. The integrating capacity of the chief executive extends to meshing the economic, technical, human, and moral dimensions of corporate activity and to relating the company to its immediate and more distant communities. It will show itself in the formal organization designs that are put into effect as the blueprint of the required structured cooperation.

The perspective demanded of successful organization leaders embraces both the primacy of organization goals and the validity of individual goals. Besides this dual appreciation, they exhibit an impartiality toward the specialized functions and have criteria enabling them to allocate organization resources against documented needs. The point of view of the leader of an organization almost by definition requires an overview of its relations not only to its internal constituencies but also to the relevant institutions and forces of its external environment. We will come soon to a conceptual solution of the problems encountered in the role of organizational leader.

Chief Executive as Personal Leader

The functions, skills, and appropriate point of view of chief executives hold true no matter who they are or who makes up their organizations. The functions that accompany performance of their role as communicator of purpose and policy, as exemplar, as the focal point for the respect or affection of subordinates vary much more according to personal energy, style, character, and integrity. Chief executives contribute as persons to the quality of life and performance in their organizations. This is true whether they are dynamic or colorless. By example they educate junior executives to seek to emulate them or simply to learn from their behavior what the chief executives really expect. They have the opportunity to infuse organized effort with flair or distinction if they have the skill to dramatize the relationship between their own activities and the goals of corporate effort.

All persons in leadership positions have or attain power that, in sophisticated organizations, they invoke as humanely and reasonably as possible in order to avoid the stultifying effects of dictatorship, dominance, or even markedly superior capacity. Formally announced policy, backed by the authority of the chief executive, can be made effective to some degree by clarity of direction, intensity of supervision, and exercise of sanctions in enforcement. But in areas of judgment where policy cannot be specified without becoming absurdly overdetailed, chief executives establish by their own demeanor, even more than in policy statements, the moral and ethical level of performance expected. At the national level of executive behavior, one could see in the deportment of Presidents Kennedy, Johnson, Nixon, and Carter how much or how little they valued ethical conduct. Failure of personal leadership in the White House leads to demoralization that is different only in scale and influence from what it is in the corporation. At the same time, however, no amount of personal integrity is sufficient without competence in organization leadership.

Formal correctness of structure and policy is not enough to inspire an organization. Enthusiasm for meeting ethical problems head-on and avoiding shoddy solutions comes not so much from a system of rewards and punishments as from the sentiments of loyalty or courage stimulated by the personal deportment of the chief executive. By the persons they are, as much as by what they say and do, presidents and CEOs influence their organizations, affect the development of individuals, and set the level of organized performance. At this juncture in the history of American business enterprise, conscious attention to the essential integrity of the chief executive becomes an important requirement if confidence in the corporate institutions of a democratic society is to be sustained and reinforced.

The skills of the effective personal leader are those of persuasion and articulation made possible by having something worth saying and by understanding the sentiments and points of view being addressed. Leaders cultivate and embody relationships between themselves and their subordinates appropriate to the style of leadership they have chosen or fallen into. Some of the qualities lending distinction to this leadership cannot be deliberately contrived, even by an artful schemer. The maintenance of personal poise in adversity or emergency and the capacity for development as an emotionally mature person are essential innate and developed capabilities. It is probably true that some personal preeminence in technical or social functions is either helpful or essential in demonstrating leadership related to the president's personal contribution. Credibility and cooperation depend upon demonstrated capacity of a kind more tangible and attractive than, for example, the noiseless coordination of staff activity.

The relevant aspects of the executive point of view brought to mind by activities in the role of personal leader are probably acknowledgment of one's personal needs and integrity as a person and acceptance of the importance to others of their own points of view, behavior, and feelings. Self-awareness will acquaint leaders with their own personal strengths and weaknesses and keep them mindful of the inevitable unevenness of their own preparation for functions of general management. These qualities may be more important in the selection of a general manager than is the study of general management.

Boards of directors in the recent past have usually followed the recommendation of their chairmen and their companies' chief executives in appointing a successor. If the CEO recommends a successor on the basis of past performance or technical competence only, without heavy weight on personal leadership capability, future organization development is put in jeopardy. The nature of modern corporate life, with new emphases on individual autonomy, voluntary cooperation, and creativity, requires strong but responsive direction. Generosity, idealism, and courage should be present in the person devoted to the company, to its view of itself, and to its innovative potential. The quarterback or the team captain, rather than the hero or autocrat, is the representative type in leading American corporations today. The choice of persons for executive position at any level once long-term strategy is apparent is probably the most important act of administration. If so, it follows that the appointment of a chief executive officer is the most crucial decision the corporate board can make.

The prototype of the chief executive that we are developing is, in short, the able victory-seeking organizational leader who is making sure in what is done and the changes pioneered in purpose and practice that the game is worth playing, the victory worth seeking, and life and career worth living. If the stature of corporation leaders as professional persons is not manifest in their concern for their organizations, they will not perform effectively over time in the role of either organization or personal leader. If we concede that the team captain should be concerned with what the game is for, we are ready to consider the role of the chief executive in the choice of corporate objectives. That choice determines what the contest is about.

Chief Executive as Architect of Purpose

To go beyond the organizational and personal roles of leadership, we enter the sphere of organization purpose, where we may find the atmosphere somewhat rare and the going less easy. The contribution senior executives make to their companies goes far beyond the apparently superficial activities that clutter their days.

Their attention to organization needs must extend beyond answering letters of complaint from spouses of aggrieved employees to appraisal, for example, of the impact of their companies' information, incentive, and control systems upon individual behavior. Their personal contribution to their company goes far beyond easily understood attention to key customers and speeches to the Economic Club to the more subtle influence their own probity and character have on subordinates. We must turn now to activities even further out—away from immediate everyday decisions and emergencies. Some part of what a president does is oriented toward maintaining the development of a company over time and preparing for a future more distant than the time horizon appropriate to the roles and functions identified thus far.

The most difficult role—and the one we will concentrate on henceforth—of the chief executive of any organization is the one in which he serves as custodian of corporate objectives. The entrepreneurs who create a company know at the outset what they are up to. Their objectives are intensely personal, if not exclusively economic, and their passions may be patent protection and finance. If they succeed in passing successfully through the phase of personal entrepreneurship, where they or their bankers or families are likely to be the only members of the organization concerned with purpose, they find themselves in the role of planner, managing the process by which ideas for the future course of the company are conceived, evaluated, fought over, and accepted or rejected.

The presidential functions involved include establishing or presiding over the goal-setting and resource-allocation processes of the company, making or ratifying choices among strategic alternatives, and clarifying and defending the goals of the company against external attack or internal erosion. The installation of purpose in place of improvisation and the substitution of planned progress in place of drifting are probably the most demanding functions of the president. Successful organization leadership requires great human skill, sensitivity, and administrative ability. Personal leadership is built upon personality and character. The capacity for determining and monitoring the adequacy of the organization's continuing purposes implies as well analytic intelligence of a high order. The chief executive we are talking about is not a two-dimensional poster or television portrait. Neither are the subordinates who help him most.

The crucial skill of the general manager concerned with corporate purpose includes the creative generation or recognition of strategic alternatives made valid by developments in the marketplace and the capability and resources of the company. Along with this, in a combination not easily come by, runs the critical capacity to analyze the strengths and weaknesses of documented proposals. The ability to perceive with some objectivity corporate strengths and weaknesses is essential to sensible choice of goals, for the most attractive goal is not attainable without the strength to open the way to it through inertia and intense opposition, with all else that lies between.

Probably the skill most nearly unique to general management, as opposed to the management of functional or technical specialties, is the intellectual capacity to conceptualize corporate purpose and the dramatic skill to invest it with some degree of magnetism. No sooner is a distinctive set of corporate objectives vividly delineated than the temptation to go beyond it sets in. Under some circumstances it is the chief executive's function to defend properly focused purpose against superficially attractive diversification or corporate growth that glitters like fool's gold. Because defense of proper strategy can be interpreted as mindless conservatism, wholly appropriate defense of a still-valid strategy requires courage, supported by detailed documentation.

Continuous monitoring, in any event, of the quality and continued suitability of corporate purpose is the most sophisticated of all the functions of general management alluded to here. Because of monitoring's difficulty and vulnerability to current emergency, you will be able to identify lost opportunities for this activity from your own experience. Everyone can. Because of its low visibility, you may not have noticed when strategic monitoring was taking place. The perspective that sustains this function is the kind of creative discontent that prevents complacency even in good times and seeks continuous advancement of corporate and individual capacity and performance. It requires also constant attention to the future, as if the present did not offer problems and opportunities enough.

Enormity of the Task

Even so sketchy a record of what a president is called upon to do is likely to seem an academic idealization, given the disparity between the complexity of role and function and the modest qualifications of those impressed into the office. Like the Molière character who discovered that for 40 years he had been speaking prose without knowing it, many managers have been programmed by instinct and experience to the kind of performance we have attempted to decipher here. For those less experienced, the catalog may seem impossibly long.

Essentially, however, we have looked at only three major roles and four sets of responsibilities. The roles deal with the requirements for organizational and personal leadership and for conscious attention to the formulation and promulgation of purpose. The four groups of functions encompass (1) securing the attainment of planned results in the present, (2) developing an organization capable of producing both technical achievement and human satisfactions, (3) making a distinctive personal contribution, and (4) planning and executing policy decisions affecting future results.

Even thus simplified, how to apply this identification of executive role and function to the incomparably detailed confusion of a national or international company situation cannot possibly be made clear in the process of generalization. But we have come to the central importance of purpose. The theory presented here begins with the assumption that in every organization (corporate or otherwise), every subunit of organization, every group and individual should be guided by evolving goals that permit movement in a chosen direction and prevent drifting in undesired directions.

Need for a Concept

The complexity of the general manager's job and the desirability of raising intuitive competence to the level of verifiable, conscious, and systematic analysis suggest the need, as indicated earlier, for a unitary concept as useful to the generalist as the canons of technical functions are to the specialist. We will propose shortly a simple practitioner's theory which we hope will reduce the four-faceted responsibility of the company's senior executives to more reasonable proportions, make that responsibility susceptible to objective research and systematic evaluation, and bring to more well-qualified people the skills it requires. The central concept we call "corporate strategy." It will be required to embrace the entire corporation, to take shape in the terms and conditions in which its business is conducted. It will be constructed from the points of view described so far. Central to this Olympian vantage point is impartiality with respect to the value of individual specialties, including the one through which the executive rose to generalist responsibilities. It will insist upon the values of the special functions in proportion to their contribution to corporate purpose and ruthlessly dispense with those not crucially related to the objectives sought. It necessarily will define the chief executive's role in such a way as to allow delegation, without loss of clarity, of much of the general management responsibility described here. Our hope will be to make challenging but practicable the connection between the highest priority for goal setting and a durable but flexible definition of a company's goals and major company-determining policies. How to define, decide, put into effect, and defend a conscious strategy appropriate to emerging market opportunity and company capability will then take precedence over and lend order to the four-fold functions of general management here presented.

Despite a shift in emphasis toward the anatomy of a concept and the development of an analytical approach to the achievement of valid corporate strategy, we will not forget the chief executive's special role in contributing quality to purpose through standards exercised in the choice of what to do and the way in which it is to be done and through the projection of *quality* as a person. It will remain true, after we have taken apart the process by which strategy is conceived, that executing it at a high professional level will depend upon the depth and durability of the chief executive's personal values, standards of quality, and clarity of character. We will return in a final comment on the management of the strategic process to the truth that the president's function above all is to be the exemplar of a permanent human aspiration—the determination to devote one's powers to jobs worth doing. Conscious attention to corporate strategy will be wasted if it does not elevate the quality of corporate purpose and achievement.

Chapter 2

The Concept of Corporate Strategy

We come at last to the simple central concept called corporate strategy. Henceforth we will be concerned with deciding what it is as idea and management process and how to formulate, evaluate, and implement it in a company. In this chapter we will examine the comprehensive definition I propose as the most useful, the terms in which strategy should be stated to make sense, the forms different kinds of strategy take in different kinds of companies, and the tests of validity that may be applied to it.

What Strategy Is

Corporate strategy is the pattern of decisions in a company that determines and reveals its objectives, purposes, or goals, produces the principal policies and plans for achieving those goals, and defines the range of business the company is to pursue, the kind of economic and human organization it is or intends to be, and the nature of the economic and noneconomic contribution it intends to make to its shareholders, employees, customers, and communities. In an organization of any size or diversity, "corporate strategy" usually applies to the whole enterprise, while "business strategy," less comprehensive, defines the choice of product or service and market of individual businesses within the firm. Business strategy is the determination of how a company will compete in a given business and position itself among its competitors. Corporate strategy defines the businesses in which a company will compete, pref-

erably in a way that focuses resources to convert distinctive competence into competitive advantage. Both are outcomes of a continuous process of strategic management that we will later examine at
length.

The strategic decision contributing to this pattern is one that is
effective over long periods of time, affects the company in many
different ways, and focuses and commits a significant portion of its
resources to the expected outcomes. The pattern resulting from a
series of such decisions will probably define the central character
and image of a company, the individuality it has for its members
and various publics, and the position it will occupy in its industry
and markets. The pattern will permit the specification of particular objectives to be attained through a timed sequence of investment and implementation decisions and will govern directly the
deployment or redeployment of resources to make these decisions
effective.

Some aspects of such a pattern of decision in an established
corporation may be unchanging over long periods of time, like a
commitment to quality, or high technology, or certain raw materials, or good labor relations. Other aspects of a strategy must
change as or before the world changes, such as product line, manufacturing process, or merchandising and styling practices. The basic determinants of company character, if purposefully institutionalized, are likely to persist through and shape the nature of substantial changes in product-market choices and allocation of
resources.

It is possible to extend the definition of strategy for a given
company to separate a central character and the core of its special
accomplishment from the manifestations of such characteristics in
changing product lines, markets, and policies designed to make
activities profitable from year to year. *The New York Times,* for
example, after many years of being shaped by the values of its
owners and staff, is now so self-conscious and respected an institution that its nature is likely to remain unchanged, even if the
services it offers are altered drastically in the direction of other
outlets for its news-processing capacity.

It is important, however, not to take the idea apart in another
way, i.e., to separate goals from the policies designed to achieve
those goals. The essence of the definition of strategy I have just
recorded is *pattern.* The interdependence of purposes, policies, and
organized action is crucial to the particularity of an individual
strategy and its opportunity to identify competitive advantage. It

is the unity, coherence, and internal consistency of a company's strategic decisions that position the company in its environment and give the firm its identity, its power to mobilize its strengths, and its likelihood of success in the marketplace. It is the interrelationship of a set of goals and policies that crystallizes, from the formless reality of a company's environment, a set of problems an organization can seize upon and solve.

We mean the term *strategy*, therefore, to suggest that *pattern* among goals is more important than any array of separate purposes. The variety of valid and attractive objectives is nearly infinite. Impressionistic selection results in uncoordinated and inefficient pursuit. Superficially attractive financial goals like high return on equity and high profit margins, for example, are in practice or at any one time incompatible with high rates of growth in sales or market share. As we will see, different kinds of objectives limit other kinds. Financial goals may impose constraints on organizational development and social goals. An organization objective of maximum decentralization will put limits on short-term attainment of cost control. The objective of continuous employment subordinates responsiveness to peaks of demand.

The interrelation among objectives is the key to coherence and consistency. The pattern of goals and policies, rather than their separate substance, is the source of the uniqueness that ideally should distinguish every company from its competitors. Especially when values visibly affect economic choices, the special character of a company becomes apparent to its employees and customers. Breaking up the system of corporate goals and the character-determining major policies for attainment leads to narrow and mechanical conceptions of strategic management and to endless logic chopping.

Many popular terms and current buzzwords refer to various aspects of goal setting. Whether you wish to think of a view of the total corporation as its *vision*, or a statement of purpose as its *mission statement*, for example, is up to you. The language for describing so central an activity as choice of purpose is infinitely varied. What is more important is to get on to understanding the need for strategic decision and for determining the most satisfactory pattern of goals in concrete instances. Refinement of definition can wait, for you will wish to develop definition in practice in directions useful to you. In the meantime, remember that what you are doing has no meaning for yourself or others unless you can sense and convey to others what you are doing it for. The quality of all administrative action and the motives lending it power cannot be understood without knowing their relationship to purpose.

Summary Statements of Strategy

Before we proceed to clarification of this concept by application, we should specify the terms in which strategy is usually expressed. A summary statement of strategy will characterize the product line and services offered or planned by the company, the markets and market segments for which products and services are now or will be designed, and the channels through which these markets will be reached. The means by which the operation is to be financed will be specified, as will the profit objectives and the emphasis to be placed on the safety of capital versus level of return. Major policy in central functions such as marketing, manufacturing, procurement, research and development, labor relations, and personnel will be stated where they distinguish the company from others, and usually the intended size, form, and climate of the organization will be included.

Each company, if it were to construct a summary strategy from what it understands itself to be aiming at, would have a different statement with different categories of decision emphasized to indicate what it wanted to be or do.

To indicate the nature of such a statement, a student of a famous old policy case on the Heublein company deduced this statement from the account of the company before it was acquired by R.J. Reynolds Industries and when it was about to make the mistake of acquiring Hamm's Brewery:

> Heublein aims to market in the U.S. and via franchise overseas a wide variety of high margin, high quality consumer products concentrated in the liquor and food business, especially bottled cocktails, vodka, and other special-use and distinctive beverages and specialty convenience foods, addressed to a relatively prosperous, young-adult market and returning over 15 percent of equity after taxes. With emphasis on the techniques of consumer goods marketing [brand promotion, wide distribution, product representation in more than one price segment, and very substantial off-beat advertising directed closely to its growing audience] Heublein intends to make Smirnoff the number one liquor brand worldwide via internal growth [and franchise] or acquisitions or both. Its manufacturing policy rather than full integration is in liquor to redistill only to bring purchased spirits up to high quality standards. It aims to finance its internal

growth through the use of debt and its considerable cash flow and to use its favorable price earnings ratio for acquisitions. Both its liquor and food distribution are intended to secure distributor support through advertising and concern for the distributor's profit.

Although it might be argued that the statement was not clearly in the chief executive's mind when he contemplated purchasing Hamm's Brewery and therefore did not help him refrain from that decision, it was in his experience and in the pattern of the company's past strategic decisions—at least as reported in the case. In many ways incomplete (no mention is made of organization or social responsibility substrategies) this statement does make possible a large question about the beer business as a compatible element in the company's marketing mix.

Reasons for Not Articulating Strategy

For a number of reasons companies seldom formulate and publish even as complete a statement as the one we have just illustrated. Conscious planning of the long-term development of companies has been until recently less common than individual executive responses to environmental pressure, competitive threat, or entrepreneurial opportunity. In the latter mode of development, the unity or coherence of corporate effort is unplanned, natural, intuitive, or even nonexistent. Incrementalism in practice sometimes gives the appearance of consciously formulated strategy, but may be the natural result of compromise among coalitions backing contrary policy proposals or skillful improvisatory adaptation to external forces. Practicing managers who prefer muddling through to the strategic process would never commit themselves to an articulate strategy.

Other reasons for the scarcity of concrete statements of strategy include the desirability of keeping strategic plans confidential for security reasons and ambiguous to avoid internal conflict or even final decision. Skillful incrementalists may have plans they do not reveal, to avoid resistance and other trouble in their own organization. A company with a large division in an obsolescent business that it intends to drain of cash until operations are discontinued could not expect high morale and cooperation to follow publication of this intent. In a dynamic company, moreover, where strategy is continually evolving, the official statement of strategy, unless it was couched in very general terms, would be as hard to

o date as an organization chart. Finally, a firm that has
:ed its strategy does not feel the need to keep saying what
iv is, ... iable as that information might be to new members.

Deducing Strategy from Behavior

In your own company you can do what most managements have not
done. In the absence of explicit statements and on the basis of your
experience, you may deduce from decisions observed what the pattern is and what the company's goals and policies are, on the
assumption that some perhaps unspoken consensus lies behind
them. Careful examination of the behavior of competitors will reveal what their strategy must be. At the same time none of us
should mistake apparent strategy visible in a pattern of past incremental decisions for conscious planning for the future. What will
pass as the current strategy of a company may almost always be
deduced from its behavior, but a strategy for a future of changed
circumstance may not always be distinguishable from performance
in the present. Strategists who do not look beyond present behavior
to the future are vulnerable to surprise.

Formulation of Strategy

Corporate strategy is an organization process, in many ways insep-
arable from the structure, behavior, and culture of the company in
which it takes place. Nevertheless, we may abstract from the process two important aspects, interrelated in real life but separable
for the purposes of analysis. The first of these we may call *formulation*, the second *implementation*. Deciding what strategy should be
may be approached as a rational undertaking, even if in life emotional attachments (as to metal skis or investigative reporting)
may complicate choice among future alternatives (for ski manufacturers or alternative newspapers). The principal subactivities of
strategy formulation as a logical activity include identifying opportunities and threats in the company's environment and attaching
some estimate or risk to the discernible alternatives. Before a
choice can be made, the company's strengths and weaknesses
should be appraised together with the resources available. Its actual or potential capacity to take advantage of perceived market
needs or to cope with attendant risks should be estimated as objectively as possible. The strategic alternative that results from
matching opportunity and corporate capability at an acceptable
level of risk is what we may call an *economic strategy*.

The process described thus far assumes that strategists are

analytically objective in estimating the relative capacity of their company and the opportunity they see or anticipate in developing markets. The extent to which they wish to undertake low or high risk presumably depends on their profit objectives. The higher they set the latter, the more willing they must be to assume a correspondingly high risk that the market opportunity they see will not develop or that the corporate competence required to excel competition will not be forthcoming.

So far we have described the intellectual processes of ascertaining what a company *might do* in terms of environmental opportunity, of deciding what it *can do* in terms of ability and power, and of bringing these two considerations together in optimal equilibrium. The determination of strategy also requires consideration of what alternatives are preferred, quite apart from economic considerations, by the chief executive and by his or her immediate associates. The acquiescence or, better, the enthusiastic engagement of all whose productivity and creativity are important in achieving superior performance grows out of participation in the process of strategic decision. Personal values, aspirations, and ideals do, and in our judgment quite properly should, influence the final choice of purposes. Thus, what the people in a company *want* to do must be brought into the strategic decision.

Finally strategic choice has an ethical aspect—a fact much more dramatically illustrated in some industries (chemicals and nuclear power, for example) than in others. Just as alternatives may be ordered in terms of the degree of risk that they entail, so may they be examined against the standards of responsiveness to the expectations of society that the strategist elects. Some alternatives may seem to the executive considering them more attractive than others when the public good or service to society is considered. What a company *should do* thus appears as a fourth element of the strategic decision.

The ability to identify the four components of strategy—(1) market opportunity, (2) corporate competence and resources, (3) personal values and aspirations, and (4) acknowledged obligations to segments of society other than stockholders—is easier to exercise than the art of reconciling their implications in a final pattern of purpose. Taken by itself each consideration might lead in a different direction.

If you put the various aspirations of individuals in your own organization against this statement you will see what I mean. Even in a single mind, contradictory aspirations can survive a long time before the need to calculate trade-offs and integrate divergent inclinations becomes clear. Growth opportunity attracted many companies to the computer business after World War II. The decision of Underwood-Olivetti to diversify out of typewriters and calculators was driven by the excitement that captivated the managements of RCA Corporation, General Electric, and Xerox Corporation, among others. But the financial, technical, and marketing requirements of this business exceeded the capacity of most of the competitors of International Business Machines Corporation (IBM). The magnet of opportunity and the incentive of desire obscured the calculations of what resources and competence were required to succeed. Where corporate capability leads, executives do not always want to go. Of all the components of strategic choice, the combination of resources and competence is most crucial to success.

The Implementation of Strategy

Because faulty implementation can make a sound strategic decision ineffective and skilled implementation can make a debatable choice successful, it is as important to examine the processes of implementation as to weigh the advantages of available strategic alternatives. The implementation of strategy is comprised of a series of subactivities that are primarily administrative. If purpose is determined, then the resources of a company can be mobilized to accomplish it. An organizational structure appropriate for the efficient performance of the required tasks must be made effective by information systems and relationships permitting coordination of subdivided activities. The organizational processes of performance measurement, compensation, management development—all of them enmeshed in systems of incentives and controls—must be directed toward the kind of behavior required by organizational purpose. The role of personal leadership is important and sometimes decisive in the accomplishment of strategy. Although we know that organization structure and processes of compensation, incentives, control, and management development influence and constrain the formulation of strategy, we should look first at the logical proposition that structure should follow strategy in order to cope later with the organizational reality that strategy also follows structure. When we have examined both tendencies, we will understand and to some extent be prepared to deal with the interdependence of the formulation and implementation of corporate purpose. Figure 1 may be useful in understanding the analysis of strategy as a pattern of interrelated decisions.

Figure 1

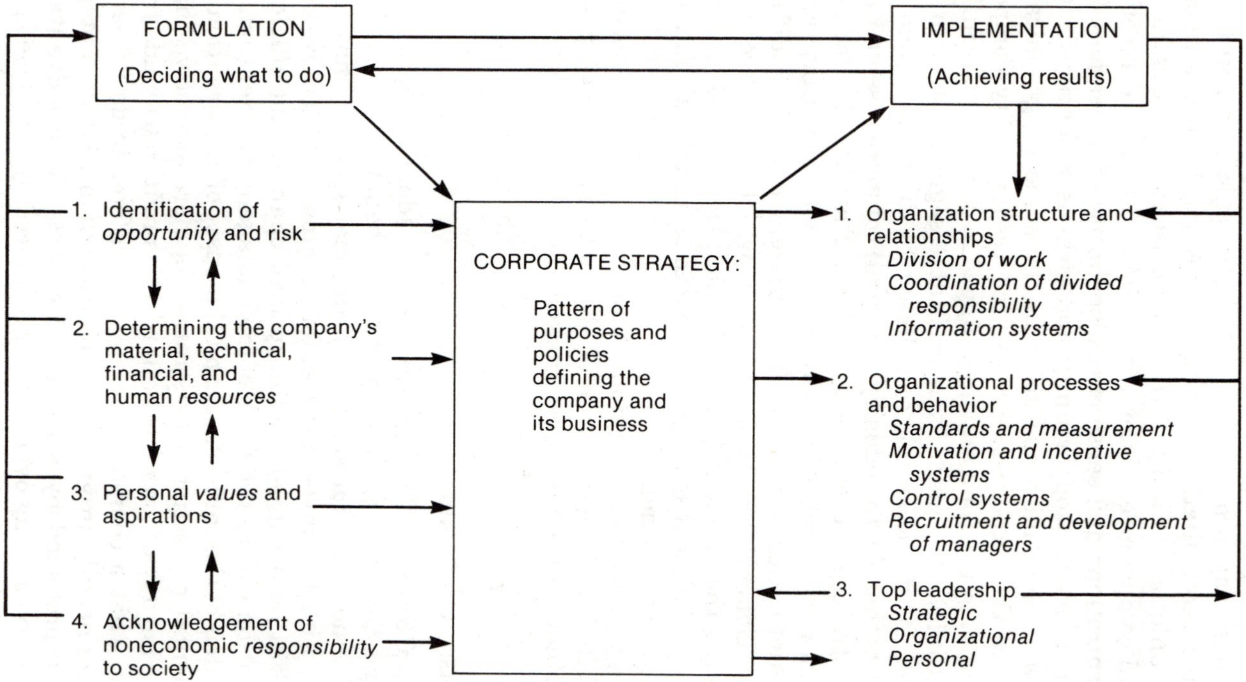

FORMULATION
(Deciding what to do)

1. Identification of
   opportunity and risk

2. Determining the company's
   material, technical,
   financial, and
   human *resources*

3. Personal *values* and
   aspirations

4. Acknowledgement of
   noneconomic *responsibility*
   to society

CORPORATE STRATEGY:

Pattern of
purposes and
policies
defining the
company and
its business

IMPLEMENTATION
(Achieving results)

1. Organization structure and
   relationships
   Division of work
   Coordination of divided
   responsibility
   Information systems

2. Organizational processes
   and behavior
   Standards and measurement
   Motivation and incentive
   systems
   Control systems
   Recruitment and development
   of managers

3. Top leadership
   Strategic
   Organizational
   Personal

Kinds of Strategies

The most important characteristic of a corporate pattern of decision that may properly be called strategic is its uniqueness. A creative reconciliation of alternatives for future development is made unique by the special characteristics of an organization, its central competence, history, financial and technical resources, and the aspirations and sense of responsibility of its leaders. The environment—market opportunity and risk—is more nearly the same for major companies operating in the same geographical regions than are the resources, values, and responsibility components of strategy. For the company unequipped to dominate the full range of opportunity, the quest for a profitable segment of, or niche in, a market is, if successful, also likely to distinguish one company from another. In an industry where all companies seem to have the same strategy, we will find trouble for all but the leaders—as at various times American Motors Corp., Chrysler Corporation, and Ford Motor Company have had different degrees of difficulty following General Motors Corporation, which got where it is by *not* following the previous industry leader, Henry Ford.

Nonetheless it is useful to have in mind the full range of possible strategies when the question is posed whether the present strategy is the best possible. When you begin to consider other possibilities, the generation of alternatives will take place within the following commonsense range of possibilities.

Low-Growth Strategies

1. No Change. The strategy properly identified and checked out against the tests of validity outlined below can be closely monitored, fine-tuned for minor defects, managed for maximum cash flows, with low investment in forced growth. Defensive contingencies will be designed for unexpected change, and efficient implementation will be the focus of top management attention. Since the recession of the mid-1970s, and the onset of conservation and environmental protection, this strategy is more attractive than it was in the heyday of "more is better." The profit to be made from doing better what a company already knows how to do rather than investing heavily in growth is the attraction of this strategy, which can be protected by achieving low costs. Its disadvantage is the possibility of being overtaken or displaced by new development and the restriction of opportunity for organization members.

2. Retreat. The possibility of liquidation is not to be sought out, but for companies in deep trouble may be a better choice than continuing the struggle. Less drastic alternatives than complete liquidation include discontinuing or divesting marginal operations or merging with a ceding of management control.

3. Focus on Limited Special Opportunity. A more constructive course of contraction is concentration on a profitable specialty product or a limited but significant market niche. Success in a narrow line almost always tempts a company to broaden its line, but the McIlhenny strategy (Tabasco sauce only) may not be totally obsolete. If the proper focus is chosen, the limits may relax and growth may come in any case. Once the risk of limited life is accepted, the advantages of the no-change strategy can be sought.

Forced-Growth Strategies

1. Acquisition of Competitors. In the early states of its development, a company with a successful strategy and proven record of successful execution can acquire small competitors in the same business to expand its market. Eventually antitrust regulation may limit this practice, unless the prospective acquisition is very small or on the edge of bankruptcy. Such acquisitions are usually followed by an adaptation of strategy either by the parent or acquired company to keep the total company a single business or one dominated by its original product-market specialization.

2. Vertical Integration. A conservative growth strategy, keeping a company close to its core competence and experience in its industry, consists of moving backward via acquisition or internal development to sources of supply and forward toward the ultimate customer. When a newspaper buys a pulp and paper mill and forest lands or news agencies for distribution, it is extending its strategy but not changing materially the nature of its business. Increasing the stages of integration provides a greater number of options to be developed or closed out as, for example, the making of fine paper and the distribution of magazines.

3. Geographical Expansion. Enlargement of territory can be accomplished by building new plants and enlarging marketing organizations or by acquiring competitors. The opportunity to enlarge international operations by export, establishment of plants and marketing activities overseas, with or without foreign partners, may protect against contraction forced by domestic competition.

4. Diversification.   The avenue to growth that presents the most difficult strategic choices is diversification. Diversification can range from minor additions to a company's basic product line to the acquisition of unrelated businesses. It can be sought through internal research and development, the purchase of new product ideas or technology, and the acquisition of companies.

Kinds of Companies

The process of strategic decision differs in complexity depending upon the diversity of the company in question. Just as having in mind the range of strategy from liquidation to multinational diversification will stimulate the generation of strategic alternatives, so a simple way of differentiating kinds of companies will help us see why different kinds of companies have different kinds of problems in making their activities coherent and effective and in setting a course for the future.

Bruce Scott of the Harvard Business School has developed a model of stages of corporate development in which each stage is characterized by the way a firm is managed and the scope of strategic choice available to it. *Stage I* is a single-product (or line of products) company with little or no formal structure run by the owner, who personally performs most of the managerial functions using subjective and unsystematic measures of performance and reward and control systems. The strategy of this firm is what the owner-manager wants it to be.

Stage II is the single-product firm grown so large that functional specialization has become imperative. A degree of integration has developed between raw materials, production processes, distribution, and sales. The search for product or process improvement is institutionalized in research and development, and performance management and control and compensation systems become systematic with the formulation of policy to guide delegation of operating decisions. The strategic choice is still under top control and centers upon the degree of integration, size of market share, and breadth of product line.

Stage III is a company with multiple product lines and channels of distribution, with an organization based on product-market relationships rather than function. Its businesses are not to a significant degree integrated; they have their own markets. Its research and development is oriented to new products rather than improvements, and its measurement and control systems are increasingly systematic and oriented to results. Strategic alternatives are phrased in terms of entry into and exit from industries, allocation of resources by industry, and rate of growth.

If a company grows it may pass from Stage I to Stage III, although it can be very large in Stage II. Its strategic decisions will grow in complexity. The stages of development model has proved productive in relating different kinds of strategies to kinds of companies and has led other researchers into productive classification. Leonard Wrigley and Richard P. Rumelt have carried Scott's work forward to develop suggestive ways of categorizing companies and comparing their strategies.[1]

First, of course, is the *single business* firm (Stages I and II firms) with 95 percent or more of its revenues arising from a single business—an oil, flour-milling, or metal container company, for example.

Second is the *dominant business* firm, diversified to some extent but still obtaining most of its revenues from a single business. The diversification may arise from end products of integration, with products stemming from strengths of the firm, or from minor unrelated activities. A large oil company in the petrochemical and fertilizer business would fall in this category.

Third is the *related business* firm in which the diversification has been principally accomplished by relating new activities to old—General Electric and Westinghouse, for example.

Fourth is the *unrelated business* firm. These firms have diversified primarily without regard to relationships between new businesses and current activities. The conglomerate companies fall in this category.

It is interesting to note that Rumelt has found significant superior performance in the related business firms, suggesting that the strategy of diversifying from the original business to a significant degree but staying within the sphere of established competence has been the most successful strategic pattern among the Fortune 500 under conditions prevailing in recent years. Unfortunately, familiar problems in establishing causation prevent final conclusions.

----

[1]Leonard Wrigley, "Division Autonomy and Diversification" (unpublished doctoral dissertation, Harvard Business School, 1970) and Richard P. Rumelt, *Strategy Structure and Economic Performance* (Division of Research, Harvard Business School, 1974). Malcolm Salter has added a refinement to Stage III in "Stages of Corporate Development," *Journal of Business Policy,* 1, no. 1 (1970), pp. 40–51.

The range of strategy and the kinds of companies that different growth strategies have produced suggest, in short, that the process of defining the business of a company will vary greatly depending on the degree of diversification under way in the company. The product-market choices are crystal clear in a single business oil company; they could not even be listed for General Electric. That top management actually decides product-market questions in such a company, except in such instances as entry into nuclear energy, is conceivable only as an oversimplification.

As diversification increases, the definition of the total business turns away from literal description of products and markets (which becomes the business of the separate product divisions) toward general statements of financial results expected and corporate principle in other areas. A conglomerate firm made up of many different businesses will have many different business strategies, related or not, depending upon the desire for synergy in the strategic direction of the total enterprise. The overall common strategy of a highly diversified firm may be only the total of its divisional strategies. That it should be more than that is a matter for argument. To make it so puts heavy demands on the ability to conceptualize corporate purpose.

The task of identifying the coherence and unity of a conglomerate is, of course, much greater than doing so for even a multidivision related business. You should be prepared, then, to adapt the beginning definition offered here to the complexity of the business you are examining. Because the trend is product diversity in growing firms and evolution from Stage I to Stage III, it is well to have this complication in mind now.

For as Norman Berg makes clear in "Strategic Planning in Conglomerate Companies," strategic choice is not merely the function of the chief executive office.[2] It is of necessity a multilevel activity, with each unit concerned with its own environment and its own objectives. The process will reflect the noneconomic goals of people at the level at which proposals are made. In a conglomerate of unrelated businesses the corporate staff is small, the division relatively autonomous, and the locus of strategic planning is in the divisions. This makes supervision of the strategic planning process and allocation of resources, depending upon the evaluation of strategies submitted, the strategic role of the corporate senior managers.

---

[2]Norman Berg, "Corporate Strategy in the Diversified Firm," Chapter 12 of his *General Management: An Analytical Approach* (Homewood, Ill.: Richard D. Irwin, Inc., 1984).

The differences in the application of a concept of strategy to a modest single business on the one hand and to a multinational conglomerate on the other—although important—mean that the ability to conceive of a business in strategic terms must be distributed throughout the organization in a complex company. The problems of choosing among strategic alternatives and making the choice effective over time, together with the problems of ensuring that such organization processes as performance measurement do not impede the choice, must be a familiar part of the management tasks of many people besides the general managers. All those involved in the strategic process, it follows, are vitally concerned with how a strategy can be evaluated so that it may be continued, amended, or abandoned as appropriate. Operating-level managers who make a strategic proposal should be able to test its validity against corporate norms if for no other reason than their own survival. Those who must approve and allocate funds to such proposals should have a criterion to evaluate their worth going beyond a general confidence (or lack of it) in the ability of the proponents.

Criteria for Evaluation

How is the actual or proposed strategy to be judged? How are we to know that one strategy is better than another? A number of important questions can regularly be asked. As is already evident, no infallible indicators are available. With practice they will lead to reliable intuitive discriminations.

1. Is the strategy identifiable and has it been made clear either in words or in practice?

The degree to which attention has been given to the strategic alternatives available to a company is likely to be basic to the soundness of its strategic decision. To cover in empty phrases ("Our policy is planned profitable growth in any market we can serve well") an absence of analysis of opportunity or actual determination of corporate strength is worse than to remain silent, for it conveys the illusion of a commitment when none has been made. The unstated strategy cannot be tested or contested and is likely therefore to be weak. If it is implicit in the intuition of a strong leader, the organization is likely to be weak and the demands the strategy makes upon it are likely to remain unmet. A strategy must be explicit to be effective and specific enough to require some actions and exclude others. Clarity should not imply rigidity.

2. Is the strategy in some way unique?

As we have already said, a fully developed strategy will visibly differentiate any company from its competitors. For producers of commodities, like chlorine or cement, the difference will not be found in the product itself but in the way it is marketed, delivered, produced, or priced. For manufacturers of proprietary products, the problem of differentiation lies in substitute products or in future direct competition when patents expire. The sameness that afflicts companies not strategically managed usually arises from industry structure, from similarities in the technology of production, and from conventions developed to limit competition, regulate market share, and educate newcomers in how things are done. Uniqueness is more the product of imagination than experience.

3. Does the strategy fully exploit domestic and international environmental opportunity?

An unqualified yes answer is likely to be rare even in the instance of such global giants as General Motors. But the present and future dimensions of markets can be analyzed without forgetting the limited resources of the company in order to outline the requirements of balanced growth and the need for environmental information. The relation between market opportunity and organizational development is a critical one in the design of future plans. Unless growth is incompatible with the resources of an organization or the aspirations of its management, it is likely that a strategy that does not purport to make full use of market opportunity will be weak also in other aspects. Vulnerability to competition is increased by lack of interest in market share.

4. Is the strategy consistent with corporate competence and resources, both present and projected?

Although additional resources, both financial and managerial, are available to companies with genuine opportunity, the availability of each must be finally determined and programmed along a practicable time scale. This may be the most difficult question in this series. The key factor which is usually left out is the availability of management for effective implementation or the opportunity cost implicit in the assignment of management to any task. It is also very difficult to assess distinctive competence, and few companies have done it to the satisfaction of more than one person.

5. Are the major provisions of the strategy and the program of major policies of which it is comprised internally consistent?

A foolish consistency, Emerson said, is the hobgoblin of little minds, and consistency of any kind is certainly not the first qualification of successful corporate CEOs. Nonetheless, one advantage of making as specific a statement of strategy as is practicable is the resultant availability of a careful check on fit, unity, coherence, compatibility, and synergy—the state in which the whole of anything can be viewed as greater than the sum of its parts. For example, a manufacturer of chocolate candy who depends for two thirds of his business upon wholesalers should not follow a policy of ignoring them or of dropping all support of their activities and all attention to their complaints. Similarly, two engineers who found a new firm expressly to do development work should not follow a policy of accepting orders that, though highly profitable, in effect turn their company into a large job shop, with the result that unanticipated financial and production problems take all the time that might have gone into development. An examination of any substantial firm will reveal at least some details in which policies pursued by different departments tend to go in different directions. Where inconsistency threatens concerted effort to achieve budgeted results within a planned time period, then consistency becomes a vital rather than merely an esthetic problem.

6. *Is the chosen level of risk feasible in economic and personal terms?*

Strategies vary in the degree of risk willingly undertaken by their designers. For example, a small food company in pursuit of its marketing strategy deliberately courted disaster in production slowdowns and in erratic behavior of cocoa futures. But the choice was made knowingly and the return was likely to be correspondingly great. The president was temperamentally able to live under this pressure and presumably had recourse if disaster struck. At the other extreme, another company had such modest growth aspirations that the junior members of its management were unhappy. They would have preferred a more aggressive and ambitious company. Although risk cannot always be known for sure, the level at which it is estimated is, within limits, optional. The riskiness of any plan should be compatible with the economic resources of the organization and the temperament of the managers concerned.

7. *Is the strategy appropriate to the personal values and aspirations of the key managers?*

Until we consider the relationship of personal values to the choice of strategy, it is not useful to dwell long upon this criterion. But, to cite an extreme case, the deliberate falsification of warehouse receipts to conceal the absence of soybean oil from the tanks that are supposed to contain it would not be an element of competitive strategy to which most of us would like to be committed. A strong personal attraction to leisure, to cite a less extreme example, is inconsistent with a strategy requiring all-out effort from the senior members of a company. Of if, for example, a new president abhors conflict and competition, then it can be predicted that the hard-driven firm of an earlier day will have to change its strategy when he takes over. Conflict between personal preferences, aspirations, and goals of the key members of an organization and the plan for its future is a sign of danger and a harbinger of mediocre performance or failure.

8. Is the strategy appropriate to the desired level of contribution to society?

Closely allied to the value is the ethical criterion. As the professional obligations of business are acknowledged by an increasing number of senior managers, it grows more and more appropriate to ask whether the current strategy of a firm is as socially responsible as it might be. Although it can be argued that filling any economic need contributes to the social good, it is clear that manufacturers of cigarettes might well consider diversification on grounds other than their fear of future legislation. That the strategy should not require violations of law or ethical practice to be effective has become abundantly clear with the revelation in the mid-1970s of widespread bribery and questionable payments, particularly in overseas activities. Honesty and integrity may seem exclusively questions of implementation, but if the strategy is not distinctive, making it effective in competition may tempt managers to unethical practice. Thus, a drug manufacturer who emphasizes the production of amphetamines at a level beyond total established medical need is inevitably compelling corruption. The meeting of sales quotas at the distribution level necessitates distribution of the drug as "speed" with or without the cooperation of prescribing physicians. To the extent that the chosen economic opportunity of the firm has social costs, such as air or water pollution, a statement of intention to deal with these is desirable and prudent. Ways to ask and answer this question will be considered in the section on the company and its responsibilities to society.

9. Does the strategy constitute a clear stimulus to organizational effort and commitment?

For organizations that aspire not merely to survive but to lead and to generate productive performance in a climate that will encourage the development of competence and the satisfaction of individual needs, the strategy selected should be examined for its inherent attractiveness to the organization. Some undertakings are inherently more likely to gain the commitment of able persons of goodwill than others. Given the variety of human preferences, it is risky to illustrate this difference briefly. But currently a company that is vigorously expanding its overseas operations finds that several of its socially conscious young people exhibit more zeal in connection with its work in developing countries than in Europe. Generally speaking, the bolder the choice of goals and the wider range of human needs they reflect, the more successfully they will appeal to the capable membership of a healthy and energetic organization.

10. Are there early indications of the responsiveness of markets and market segments to the strategy?

Results, no matter how long postponed by necessary preparations, are the most telling indicators of soundness, as long as they are read correctly at the proper time. A strategy may pass with flying colors all the tests so far proposed and may be in internal consistency and uniqueness an admirable work of art. But if within a time period made reasonable by the company's resources and the original plan the strategy does not work, then it must be weak in some way that has escaped attention. Bad luck, faulty implementation, and competitive countermoves may be more to blame for unsatisfactory results than flaws in design, but the possibility of the latter should not be unduly discounted. Conceiving a strategy that will win the company a unique place in the business community, give it an enduring concept of itself, harmonize its diverse activities, and provide a fit between environmental opportunity and present or potential company strength is an extremely complicated task. The idea of strategy becomes complex in its application.

We cannot expect simple tests of soundness to deliver a complete evaluation. But an analytical examination of any company's strategy against the several criteria here suggested will give anyone concerned with the quality of corporate planning more than enough to think about.

Problems in Evaluation

The evaluation of strategy is as much an act of judgment as is the original conception and may be as subject to error. The most common source of difficulty is the misevaluation of current results. When results are unsatisfactory, as we have just pointed out, a reexamination of strategy is called for. At the same time, outstandingly good current results are not necessarily evidence that the strategy is sound. Abnormal upward surges in demand may deceive marginal producers that all is well within their current strategy, until expansion of more efficient competitors wipes out their market share. Extrapolation of present performance into the future, overoptimism and complacence, and underestimation of competitive response and of the time required to accommodate to changes in demand are often by-products of success. Unusually high profits may blind the unwary manager to impending environmental change. His concern for the future can under no circumstances be safely suspended. Conversely, a high-risk strategy that has failed was not necessarily a mistake, so long as the risk was anticipated and the consequences of failure carefully calculated. In fact, a planning problem confronting a number of diversified companies today is how to encourage their divisions to undertake projects where failure can be afforded but where success, if it comes, will be attended by high profits not available in run-of-the-mill, low-risk activities.

Although the possibility of misinterpreting results is by far the commonest obstacle to accurate evaluation of strategy, the criteria previously outlined suggest immediately some additional difficulties. It is as easy to misevaluate corporate resources and the financial requirements of a new move as to misread the environment for future opportunities. To be overresponsive to industry trends may be as dangerous as to ignore them. The correspondence of the company's strategy with current environmental developments and an overreadiness to adapt may obscure the opportunity for a larger share of a declining market or for growth in profits without a parallel growth in total sales.

The intrinsic difficulty of determining and choosing among strategic alternatives leads many companies to do what the rest of the industry is doing rather than to make an independent determination of opportunity and resources. Sometimes the companies of an industry run like sheep all in one direction. The similarity among the strategies, at least in some periods of history, of insurance companies, banks, railroads, and airplane manufacturers may lead one to conclude that strategic decisions were based on industry convention more than on independent analysis.

A strategy may manifest an all-too-clear correspondence with the personal values of the founder, owner, or chief executive. Like a correspondence with dominant trends and the strategic decisions of competitors, this one may also be deceptive and unproductive. For example, a personal preference for growth beyond all reasonable expectations may be given undue weight. It should be only one factor among several in any balanced consideration of what is involved in designing strategy. Too little attention to a corporation's actual competence for growth or diversification is the commonest error of all.

It is entirely possible that a strategy may reflect in an exaggerated fashion the values rather than the reasoned decisions of the responsible manager or managers. That imbalance may go undetected. The entire business community may be dominated by certain beliefs of which one should be wary. A critic of strategy must be at heart enough of a nonconformist to raise questions about generally accepted modes of thought and conventional thinking that substitutes for original analysis. The timid may not find it prudent to challenge publicly some of the ritual of policy formulation. But even for them it will serve the purposes of criticism to inquire privately into such sacred propositions as the one proclaiming that a company must grow or die or that national planning for world competitiveness is anathema.

Another canon of management that may engender questionable strategies is the idea that cash funds in excess of reasonable dividend requirements should be reinvested whether in revitalization of a company's traditional activities or in mergers and acquisitions that will diversify products and services. Successful operations, a heretic might observe, sometimes bring riches to a company that lacks the capacity to reemploy them. Yet a decision to return to the owners substantial amounts of capital which the company does not have the competence or desire to put to work is an almost unheard-of development. It is therefore appropriate, particularly in the instance of very successful companies in older and stable industries, to inquire how far strategy reflects a simple desire to put all resources to work rather than a more valid appraisal of investment opportunity in relation to unique corporate strengths. We should not forget to consider an unfashionable, even if ultimately also an untenable, alternative—namely, that to keep an already large worldwide corporation within reasonable bounds, a portion of the assets might well be returned to stockholders for investment in other enterprises.

Much more serious misevaluation of strategy stems from a pervasive conflict between the academic interests of financial economics and the practitioner orientation of the concept of corporate strategy. The use of simple ratios like the relation of debt to equity or simple measures like return on investment, return on equity, or earnings per share as determinants of decision often lead to short-sighted moves to satisfy a measure rather than to make a strategic investment. (The related misuse of portfolio analysis leads similarly to mechanical appraisal of separate businesses rather than relating the separate businesses to the future of the company as a whole.) Capital budgeting that applies discounted cash flow analysis ignores the difficulties of estimating discount rates, future cash flows, and the project's impact on the company's cash flow from other assets and on the firm's future investment opportunities.

The distortion in evaluating and shaping strategy by overuse of financial formulas and rules of thumb is unwittingly perpetrated by financial analysts, financial economists, and students of financial theory who appear unaware of the need to make financial policy serve, rather than dominate, corporate strategy. Parochial use of financial expertise can pervert the strategic process by appearing to justify project-by-project rather than strategy-dominated decisions. Such perversion originates in the simplistic assumption (with implicit emphasis on the short term) that the single purpose of corporate enterprise is the enhancement of shareholder wealth.

The identification of opportunity and choice of purpose are such challenging intellectual activities that we should not be surprised to find that persistent problems attend the proper evaluation of strategy. But just as the criteria for evaluation are useful, even if not precise, so the dangers of misevaluation are less menacing if they are recognized. We have noted some inexactness in the concept of strategy, the problems of making resolute determinations in the face of uncertainty, the necessity for judgment in the evaluation of soundness of strategy, and the misevaluation into which human error may lead us. None of these alters the commonsense conclusion that a business enterprise guided by a clear sense of purpose rationally arrived at and emotionally ratified by commitment is more likely to have a successful outcome, in terms of profit and social good, than a company whose future is left to guesswork and chance. Conscious strategy does not preclude brilliance of improvisation or the welcome consequences of good fortune. Its cost is principally thought and work for which it is hard but not impossible to find time.

Chapter 3

The Company and Its Environment: Relating Opportunities to Resources

Determination of a suitable strategy for a company begins in identifying the opportunities and risks in its environment. This chapter is concerned with the identification of a range of strategic alternatives, the narrowing of this range by recognizing the constraints imposed by corporate capability, and the determination of one or more economic strategies at acceptable levels of risk. We shall examine the complexity and variety of the environmental forces that must be considered and the problems in accurately assessing company strengths and weaknesses. Economic strategy will be seen as the match between qualification and opportunity that positions a firm in its product-market environment. We shall attempt to categorize the kinds of economic strategies that can result from the combination of internal capability and external market needs, and to relate these categories to the normal course of corporate development.

The Nature of the Company's Environment

The environment of a business organization, like that of any other organic entity, is the pattern of all the external conditions and influences that affect its life and development. The environmental influences relevant to strategic decision operate in a company's industry, the total business community, its city, its country, and the world. They are technological, economic, physical, social, and political. The corporate strategist is usually at least intuitively aware of these features. But in all these categories change is taking place at varying rates—fastest in technology, less rapidly in politics. Change in the environment of business necessitates continuous monitoring of a company's definition of its business, lest it falter, blur, or become obsolete. Because by definition strategy is formulated with the future in mind, executives who take part in the strategic planning process must be aware of those aspects of their company's environment especially susceptible to the kind of change that will affect their company's future.

Technology. From the point of view of the corporate strategist, technological developments are not only the fastest unfolding but also the most far-reaching in extending or contracting opportunity for an established company. These developments include the discoveries of science, the impact of related product development, the less dramatic machinery and process improvements, and the progress of automation and data processing. We see generally in technical advance an accelerating rate of change—with new developments arriving before the implications of yesterday's changes can be assimilated. Industries hitherto protected from obsolescence by stable technologies or by the need for huge initial capital investment become more vulnerable more quickly than before to new processes or to cross-industry competition. Periodic lulls do occur to slow the velocity of technical development. Recession, inflation, high interest rates, and dislocations in energy costs at times divert entrepreneurial drive and government and business investment in research and development to cost reduction and process improvement and to defensive inaction in general. The stubbornness of the major problems still unsolved (for example, solar energy, cancer, or air pollution) leaves research apparently plateaued from time to time. In view of world competition, however, national policy and corporate drive will not long permit such slowdowns in technical development as seemed to occur as the 1970s came to a close. Science, which does not pause, gives impetus to change not only in technology but also in all other aspects of business activity.

Major areas of technical advance foreseen by students of the management of technology include the conservation and more efficient use of energy, the reorganization of transportation, technical solutions to problems of product life, safety, and serviceability, the further mechanization of logistical functions and the processing of information, alteration in the characteristics of physical and biological materials, and radical developments in controlling air, water, and noise pollution. The primary impact upon established strategies will be increased competition and more rapid obsolescence. The risks dramatized by these technical trends are offset by new business opportunities opened up for companies that are aggressive innovators or adept at technical hitchhiking. The need intensifies for any company either to engage in technical development or to maintain a technical intelligence capability enabling it to follow quickly new developments pioneered by others.

Ecology. It used to be possible to take for granted the environment's physical characteristics and find them favorable to industrial development. Plant sites were chosen using criteria like availability of process and cooling water, accessibility to various forms of transportation, and stability of soil conditions. With the increase in sensitivity to the impact on the physical environment of all industrial activity, it becomes essential, both to comply with law and behave responsibly, to consider how planned expansion and even continued operation under changing standards will affect and be perceived to affect the air, water, traffic density, and quality of life of any area that a company would like to enter. The trade-off between economic production and preservation or improvement of the ecological status quo has been dramatically revealed in the use of plentiful high-sulfur coal in the generation of electric power. Predictions involving high risk must be made about how such trade-offs will be resolved in the ebb and flow of public opinion.

Economics. Because business is more accustomed to monitoring economic trends than those in other spheres, it is less likely to be taken by surprise by such massive developments as the internationalization of competition, the opportunity in China and Russia for trade with the West, the slower than projected development of the Third World countries, the Americanization of demand and culture in the developing countries and the resulting backlash of nationalism, the increased importance of the large multinational corporations and the consequences of host-country hostility, the recurrence of recession, and the threat of renewed inflation. The consequences of world economic trends need to be monitored in much greater detail for any one industry or company than was once necessary.

Industry. Although the industry environment is the one most company strategists believe they know most about, the opportunities and risks that reside there are often blurred by familiarity and the uncritical acceptance of the established relative position of competitors. Michael Porter,[1] in an effort to develop strategically useful analysis of the structure of industries, has decided the nature of competition in an industry and its profit potential are affected by certain structural determinants—the threat of entry by new firms, the relative power of suppliers and customers, and the development of substitute products by other industries. Whether an industry is fragmented, emerging, maturing, or declining affects strategic opportunity as much as whether it produces basic commodities or products reflecting rapid technological change.

A close look at any industry will reveal its strategic dimensions and the strategic groups consisting of companies that have made similar decisions about these dimensions. Strategy formulation in this view becomes a decision of which strategic group to compete in, without precluding the preservation of competitive advantage within the group. Reading market signals consciously or unconsciously offered by competitors gives clues to competitors' motives, goals, internal situations, and intentions. The strategic significance of changes in industry structure as it evolves around competitors' jockeying for position should be determined in the firm's search for opportunity in the total environment.

Society. Social developments of which strategists keep aware include such influential forces as the quest for equality for minority groups, the demand of women for opportunity and recognition, the changing patterns of work and leisure, the effects of urbanization upon the individual, family, and neighborhood, the rise of crime, the decline of conventional morality, and the changing composition of world population.

Politics. The political forces important to the business firm are similarly extensive and complex—the changing relations between communist and noncommunist countries (East and West) and between prosperous and poor countries (North and South), the relation between private enterprise and government and between workers and management, the impact of national planning on corporate planning, and the rise of what George Lodge calls the communitarian ideology.[2] The amount of time chief strategic officers of sizable corporations must spend in legislative committees consider-

---

[1]Michael E. Porter, *Competitive Strategy: Techniques for Analyzing Industries and Competitors* (New York: Free Press, 1980). See also his *Competitive Advantage* (New York: Free Press, 1985).

[2]George C. Lodge, *The New American Ideology* (New York: Alfred A. Knopf, Inc., 1975) and *The American Disease* (New York: Alfred A. Knopf, Inc., 1984).

ing proposals for corporate governance increases steadily. Such exposure should equip corporate leadership to anticipate public concern and take it into account in making strategic decisions.[3]

Although it is not possible to know or spell out here the significance of such technical, economic, social, and political trends and possibilities for the strategist of a given business or company, some simple things are clear. Changing values will lead to different expectations of the role business should perform. Business will be expected to execute its mission not only with economy in the use of energy but with sensitivity to the ecological environment. Organizations in all walks of life will be called upon to be more explicit about their goals and to meet the needs and aspirations (for example, for education) of their membership.

In any case, change threatens all established strategies, including those currently successful. We know that a thriving company— itself a living system—is bound up in a variety of interrelationships with larger systems comprising its technological, economic, ecological, social, and political environment. If environmental developments are destroying and creating business opportunities, advance notice of specific instances relevant to a single company is essential to intelligent planning. Risk and opportunity in the last dozen years of the 20th century require of executives a keen interest in what is going on outside their companies. More than that, a practical means of tracking developments promising good or ill and profit or loss needs to be devised.

Tracking the Changing Environment

Unfortunately the development of knowledge in a flourishing business civilization has produced no easy methodology for continuous surveillance of the environmental trends of central importance to a firm of ordinary capabilities. Predictive theories of special disciplines such as economics, sociology, psychology, and anthropology do not produce comprehensive appraisal readily applicable to long-range corporate strategic decision. At the same time many techniques do exist to deal with parts of the problem—economic and technological forecasting, detailed demographic projections, geological estimates or raw material reserves, and national and international statistics in which trends may be discerned. More information about the environment is available than is commonly used.

---

[3]See Irving S. Shapiro, *America's Third Revolution* (New York: Harper & Row, 1984) for an enlightened redefinition of the interdependence of business and government.

The underuse of technical information has continued unchanged since Aguilar's research in how managers in the chemical
industry obtained strategic information about environmental
change.[4] Aguilar found that even in this technically sensitive industry, few firms attempted any systematic means for gathering
and evaluating such information. Publications provided only about
20 percent of the information from all sources, with current market
and competitive information from personal sources dominating the
total input of information. Internally generated information comprised only 9 percent of the total, and more information received
was unsolicited than solicited. (Interestingly, very few people in
subordinate positions believed they were getting useful strategic
information from their superiors.)

Aguilar's findings have been corroborated by studies in other
industries. The obvious moral of these studies is that the process of
obtaining strategic information is far from being systematic, complete, or even really informative about anything except current
developments. This research shows it is possible to better organize
the gathering and integrating of environmental data through such
means as bringing miscellaneous scanning activities together and
communicating available information internally.

We should not be carried away by this possibility, for limitations of time, interest, and willpower will no doubt continue to
leave word of mouth, coalescing occasionally to establish conventional wisdom, the dominant mode of communication among senior
managers, who are often accused of thinking very much alike. This
human tendency occasionally presents opportunities for the strategists who, out of originality or perversity, decide the opposite of
what they hear is the truth.

Certain large companies organize a disciplined inquiry to un-
dergird the assumptions of their leaders about the future. General
Electric once maintained a Business Environment Section at its
corporate headquarters. It prepared reports on predicted changes
for use by GE divisions. Consulting firms, future-oriented research
organizations, and associations of planners provide guidance for
looking ahead.

Electronically accessible data bases have proliferated beyond
the ability to make use of them. The sense of futility experienced
by executives in the face of overabundant information is reduced
when they begin the task by defining their strategy and the most
likely strategic alternatives they will be debating in the foresee-

---

[4]Frank J. Aguilar, *Scanning the Business Environment* (New York: The Mac-
millan Company, 1967).

able future. Decision on direction spotlights the relevant environment. You cannot know everything, but if you are thinking of going into the furniture business in Nebraska you will not be immoderately concerned about the rate of family formation in Japan. Clarification of present strategy and the few new alternatives it suggests narrows sharply the range of necessary information and destroys the excuse that there is too much to know.

Identification of Opportunities and Risks

For the firm that has not determined what its strategy dictates it needs to know or has not embarked upon the systematic surveillance of environmental change, a few simple questions kept constantly in mind will highlight changing opportunity and risk. In examining your own company or one you are interested in, these questions should lead to an estimate of opportunity and danger in the present and predicted company setting.

1. What are the essential economic, technical, and structural characteristics of the industry in which the company participates?

Whether these are in flux or not, such characteristics may define the restrictions and opportunities confronting the individual company and will certainly suggest strategy. For example, knowledge that the cement industry requires high investment in plant, proximity to certain raw materials, a relatively small labor force, and enormous fuel and transportation costs suggests where to look for new plant sites and what will constitute competitive advantage and disadvantage. The nature of its product may suggest for a given company the wisdom of developing efficient pipeline and truck transportation and cheaper energy sources rather than engaging in extensive research to achieve product differentiation or aggressive price competition to increase its market share.

2. What trends suggesting future change in economic and technical characteristics are apparent?

Changes in demand for the product of one industry in competition with the products of another and changes in the product itself occurring as a result of research and development affect the chance for growth. For example, the glass container industry's development years ago of strong, light, disposable bottles and more recently combinations of glass and plastic recouped part of the market lost by glass to the metal container. The glass industry's need for this development was made apparent by the success of the metal beer can. Similarly, the easy-opening metal container suggested the need for an easily removable bottle cap. The physical characteristics of any product can be examined against the master trend toward simplicity, convenience, and serviceability in consumer goods and against competitive innovations. Both the glass bottle and the metal container face increasingly effective attack by environmentalists, who constitute a noneconomic and nontechnical force to be reckoned with. Container industries should have begun long ago, for example, to develop logistical solutions to the legislatively mandated returnable bottle and can.

3. What is the nature of competition both within the industry and across industries?

A small rubber company, in an industry led by Goodyear Tire & Rubber Company, will not, under the economic condition of overcapacity, elect to provide the automobile business with original tires for new cars. The structure of competition, quite apart from the resources of the firm, may suggest that a relatively small firm should seek out a niche of relatively little interest to the major companies and concentrate its powers on that limited market segment.

Present and developing competition usually extends, of course, beyond the industry in which a company finds itself. For example, the competition for the cement industry from producers of asphalt road-building materials is as important as that from other cement producers.

4. What are the requirements for success in competition in the company's industry?

In every industry some critical tasks must be performed particularly well to ensure survival. In the ladies' belt and handbag business, style and design are critical, but so (less obviously) are relationships with department store buyers. In the computer business, a sales force able to diagnose customer requirements for information systems, to design a suitable system, and to equip a customer to use it is more important than the circuitry of hardware. Thus, the development of software, long neglected by the manufacturers of machines, has finally been recognized as critical. The integration of input devices, terminals, file and memory banks, copiers and printers constitutes the real battleground.

Although the question of what tasks are most critical may be chiefly useful as a means of identifying risks or possible causes of failure, it may also suggest opportunity. Imagination in perceiving new requirements for success under changing conditions, when production-oriented competitors have not done so, can give a company leadership position. For example, opportunity for a local radio station and the strategy it needed to follow changed sharply with the rise of television, and those who first diagnosed the new requirements paid much less for radio stations than was later necessary.

5. Given the technical, economic, social, and political developments that most directly apply, what is the range of strategy available to any company in this industry?

The force of this question is obvious in the drug industry. The speed and direction of pharmaceutical research, the structure of the industry, the characteristics of worldwide demand, the different and changing ideas about how adequate medical care should be made available to the world's population, the concern about price, and the nature of government regulation suggest constraints within which a range of opportunity is still vividly clear. Similarly, in a more stable industry, there is always a choice. To determine the limits of choice, an examination of environmental characteristics and developments is essential.

Opportunity as a Determinant of Strategy

Awareness of the environment is not a special project to be undertaken only when warning of change becomes deafening; it is a continuing requirement for informed choice of purpose. Planned exploitation of changing opportunity ordinarily follows a predictable course that provides increasing awareness of areas to which a company's capabilities may be profitably extended. A useful way to perceive the normal course of development is to use Bruce Scott's stages referred to briefly above.

The manufacturer of a single product (Stage I) sold within a clearly defined geographical area to meet a known demand finds it relatively easy to identify opportunity and risk. As an enterprise develops a degree of complexity requiring functional division or management decision, it encounters, as an integrated Stage II company, a number of strategic alternatives in its market environments that the Stage I proprietor is too hard-pressed to notice and almost too overcommitted to consider. Stage III companies, deployed along the full range of diversification, find even a greater number of possibilities for serving a market profitably than the resources they possess or have in sight will support. The more one finds out what might be done, the harder it is to make the final choice.

The diversified Stage III company has another problem different from that of trying to make the best choice among many. If it has divisionalized its operations and strategies, as sooner or later in the course of diversification it must, then divisional opportunities compete with each other. Strategy formulation and environmental surveillance become organization processes.

The corporate management normally will wish to invest profits not distributed to stockholders in those opportunities that will produce the greatest return to the corporation. If need be, corporate management, after portfolio analysis, will be willing to let an individual division decline if its future looks less attractive than that of others. The division, on the other hand, will wish to protect its own market position, ward off adverse development, prolong its own existence, and provide for its growth. The division manager, who is not rewarded for failures, may program projects of safe but usually not dramatic prospects. The claims regarding projected return on investment, which are submitted in all honesty as the divisional estimate of future opportunity, can be assumed to be biased by the division's regard for its own interest and the manager's awareness of measurement.

The corporate management cannot be expected to be able to make independent judgments about all the proposals for growth submitted by all the divisions. On the other hand, all divisions cannot be given their heads, if the corporation's needs for present profit are to be met and if funds for reinvestment are limited. In any case, the greatest knowledge about the opportunities for a given technology and set of markets should be found at the divisional level.

The strategic dilemma of a conglomerate world enterprise is the most complex in the full range of policy decisions. When the variety of what must be known cannot be reduced by a sharply focused strategy to the capacity of a single mind and when the range of a company's activities spans many industries and technologies, the problems of formulating a coherent strategy begin to get out of hand. Here strategy must become a managed process rather than the decision of the chief executive officer and his immediate associates. Bower and Prahalad have shown in important research how the context of decision can be controlled by the top management group and how power can be distributed through a hierarchy to influence the kind of strategic decision that will survive in the system.[5] The process of strategic decision can, like complex opera-

---

[5] Joseph L. Bower, *Managing the Resource Allocation Process* (Boston: Harvard Business School Press, 1986), and C.K. Prahalad, "Strategic Choices in Diversified MNCs," *Harvard Business Review* (July-August 1976), pp. 67–78. See also Norman Berg and Robert A. Pitts, "Strategic Management: The Multi-Business Corporation," in Dan E. Schendel and Charles W. Hofer, *Strategic Management* (Boston, Mass.: Little Brown & Co., 1979).

tions, be organized in such a way as to provide appropriate complementary roles for decentralization and control.

To conceive of a new development in response to market information and prediction of the future is a creative act. To commit resources to it only on the basis of projected return and the estimate of probability constituting risk of failure is foolhardy. More than economic analysis of potential return is required for decision because economic opportunity abounds far beyond the ability to capture it. That money might be made in a new field or growth industry does not mean a company with abilities developed in a different field is going to make it. We turn now to the critical factors that make one opportunity better than another for an individual company.

Identifying Corporate Competence and Resources

The first step in validating a tentative choice among several opportunities is to determine whether the organization has the capacity to prosecute it successfully. The capability of an organization is its demonstrated and potential ability to accomplish, against the opposition of circumstance or competition, whatever it sets out to do. Every organization has actual and potential strengths and weaknesses. Because it is prudent in formulating strategy to extend or maximize the one and contain or minimize the other, it is important to try to determine what they are and to distinguish one from the other.

It is just as possible, though much more difficult, for a company to know its own strengths and limitations as it is to maintain a workable surveillance of its changing environment. Subjectivity, lack of confidence, and unwillingness to face reality may make it hard for organizations and individuals to know themselves. But just as it is essential, though difficult, that a maturing person achieve reasonable self-awareness, so an organization can identify approximately its central strength and critical vulnerability.

Howard H. Stevenson a decade ago made the first formal study of management practice in defining corporate strengths and weaknesses as part of the strategic planning process.[6] He looked at five aspects of the process: (1) the attributes of the company that its managers examined, (2) the organizational scope of the strengths and weaknesses identified, (3) the measurement employed in the

---

[6]Howard H. Stevenson, "Defining Corporate Strengths and Weaknesses: An Exploratory Study," *Sloan Management Review* (Spring 1976).

process of definition, (4) the criteria for telling a strength from a weakness, and (5) the sources of relevant information. As might be expected, the process Stevenson was looking at was imperfectly and variously practiced in the half dozen companies he studied. He found that the problems of defining corporate strengths and weaknesses, very different from those of other planning processes, center mostly upon a general lack of agreement on suitable definition, criteria, and information. Stevenson's most important conclusion is that the attempt to define strengths and weaknesses is more useful than the usual final product of the process.

Stevenson's exploratory study in no way diminishes the importance of trying to appraise organization capability. Such appraisal protects against oversimplification. The absence of criteria and measures, the disinclination for appraising competence except in relation to specific problems, the uncertainty about what is meant by "strength" and "weakness," and the reluctance to imply criticism of individuals or organizational subunits—all these hampered his study but illuminated the problem. Much of what is intuitive in this process is yet to be identified. Essential to effective membership in an organization is the capacity as an individual to see through the loyalty he or she feels to its objectively ascertainable capabilities.

To make an effective contribution to strategic planning, the key attributes to be appraised should be identified and consistent criteria established for judging them. If attention is directed to strategies, policy commitments, and past practices in the context of discrepancy between organization goals and attainment, an outcome useful to an individual manager's strategic planning is possible. The assessment of strengths and weaknesses associated with the attainment of specific objectives becomes, in Stevenson's words, a "key link in a feedback loop" that allows managers to learn from the success or failures of the policies they institute.

While this study does not find or establish a systematic way of developing or using such knowledge, members of organizations do develop judgments about what the company can do particularly well—its core of competence. If consensus can be reached about this capability, no matter how subjectively arrived at, its application to identified opportunity can be estimated.

Sources of Capabilities.   The powers of a company constituting resources for growth and diversification accrue primarily from experience in making and marketing a product line or providing a service. They inhere as well in (1) the developing strengths and weaknesses of the individuals comprising the organization, (2) the degree to which individual capability is effectively applied to the common task, and (3) the quality of coordination of individual and group effort.

The experience gained through successful execution of a strategy centered upon one goal may unexpectedly develop capabilities that could be applied to different ends. Whether they should be so applied is another question. For example, a manufacturer of salt can strengthen his competitive position by offering his customers salt-dispensing equipment. If, in the course of making engineering improvements in this equipment, a new solenoid principle is perfected that has application to many industrial switching problems, should this patentable and marketable innovation be exploited? The answer would depend not only on whether economic analysis of the opportunity shows this to be a durable and profitable possibility, but also on whether the organization can muster the financial, manufacturing, and marketing strength to exploit the discovery and live with its success. The former question is likely to have a more positive answer than the latter. In this connection, it seems important to remember that individual and unsupported flashes of strength are not as dependable as the gradually accumulated product and market-related fruits of experience.

Even where competence to exploit an opportunity is nurtured by experience in related fields, the level of that competence may be too low for any great reliance to be placed upon it. Thus, a chain of children's clothing stores might well acquire the administrative, merchandising, buying, and selling skills that would permit it to add departments in women's wear. Similarly, a sales force effective in distributing typewriters might gain proficiency in selling office machinery and supplies. But even here it would be well to ask what *distinctive* ability these companies could bring to the retailing of soft goods or office equipment to attract customers away from a plethora of competitors.

Identifying Strengths.   The distinctive competence of an organization is more than what it can do; it is what it can do particularly well. To identify the less obvious or by-product strengths of an organization that may well be transferable to some more profitable new opportunity, one might begin by examining the organization's current product line and by defining the functions it serves in its markets. Almost any important consumer product has functions that are related to others into which a qualified company might move. The typewriter, for example, is more than the simple machine for mechanizing handwriting that it once appeared to be when looked at only from the point of view of its designer and manufacturer. Closely analyzed from the point of view of the potential user, the typewriter is found to contribute to a broad range of information-processing functions. Any one of these might have suggested an area to be exploited by a typewriter manufacturer. Tacitly defining a typewriter as a replacement for a fountain pen as a writing instrument rather than as an input-output device for word processing is the explanation provided by hindsight for the failure of the old-line typewriter companies to develop before IBM did the electric typewriter and the computer-related input-output devices it made possible. The definition of product that would lead to identification of transferable skills must be expressed in terms of the market needs it may fill rather than the engineering specifications to which it conforms.

Besides looking at the uses or functions to which present products contribute, the would-be diversifier might profitably identify the skills that underlie whatever success has been achieved. The qualifications of an organization efficient at performing its long-accustomed tasks come to be taken for granted and considered humdrum, like the steady provision of first-class service. The insight required to identify the essential strength justifying new ventures does not come naturally. Its cultivation can probably be helped by recognizing the need for analysis. In any case, we should look beyond the company's capacity to invent new products. Because product leadership is not possible for a majority of companies it is fortunate that patentable new products are not the only major highway to new opportunities. Other avenues include new marketing services, new methods of distribution, new values in quality-price combinations, and creative merchandising.[7] The effort to find or to create a competence that is truly distinctive may hold the real key to a company's success or even to its future development. For example, the ability of a cement manufacturer to run a truck fleet more effectively than its competitors may constitute one of its principal competitive strengths in selling an undifferentiated product.

Matching Opportunity and Competence.   The way to narrow the range of alternatives, made extensive by imaginative identification of new possibilities, is to match opportunity to competence, once each has been accurately identified and its future significance estimated. It is this combination that establishes a company's economic mission and its position in its environment. The combina-

---

[7]See Theodore Levitt, "Marketing Success through Differentiation—of Anything," *Harvard Business Review* (January-February 1980), pp. 83 ff.

tion is designed to minimize organizational weakness and to maximize strength. In every case, risk attends it. And when opportunity seems to outrun present distinctive competence, the willingness to gamble that the latter can be built up to the required level is almost indispensable to a strategy that challenges the organization and the people in it. Figure 2 diagrams the matching of opportunity and resources that results in an economic strategy.

Before we leave the creative act of putting together a company's unique internal capability and opportunity evolving in the external world, we should note that—aside from distinctive competence—the principal resources found in any company are money and people—technical and managerial people. At an advanced stage of economic development, money seems less a problem than technical competence, and the latter less critical than managerial ability. Do not assume that managerial capacity can rise to any occasion. The diversification of American industry is marked by hundreds of instances in which a company strong in one endeavor lacked the ability to manage an enterprise requiring different skills. The right to make handsome profits over a long period must be earned. Opportunism without competence is hollow.

Besides equating an appraisal of market opportunity and organizational capability, the decision to make and market a particular product or service should be accompanied by an identification of the nature of the business and the kind of company its management desires. Such a guiding concept is a product of many considerations, including the managers' personal values. As such, this concept will change more slowly than other aspects of the organization, and it will give coherence to all the company activities. For example, a president who is determined to make his or her firm into a worldwide producer and fabricator of a basic metal, through policies differentiating it from the industry leader, will not be distracted by excess capacity in developed markets, by low metal prices, and by cutthroat competition in certain markets. Such a firm would not be sidetracked into acquiring, for example, the Pepsi-Cola franchise in Africa, even if this business promised to yield a good profit. (That such a firm should have an experimental division exploring offshoot technology is, however, entirely appropriate.)

Uniqueness of Strategy. In each company, the way in which distinctive competence, organizational resources, and organizational values are combined is or should be unique. Differences among companies are as numerous as differences among individuals. The combinations of opportunity to which distinctive compe-

Figure 2

Schematic Development of Economic Strategy

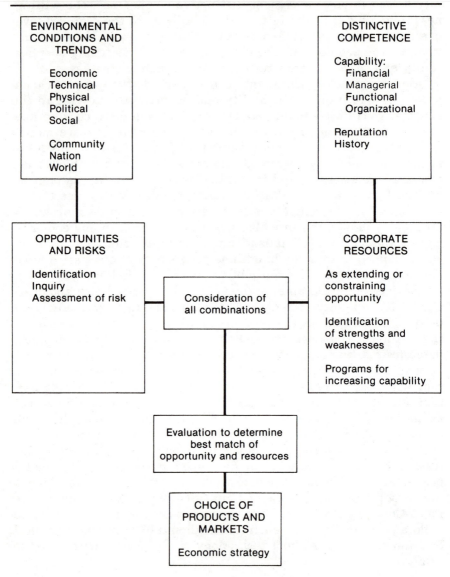

tences, resources, and values may be applied are equally extensive. Generalizing about how to make an effective match is less rewarding than working at it. The effort is a highly stimulating and challenging exercise. The outcome will be unique for each company and each situation.

Application to Situations

Because all these observations do not bear fruit until their potency is tested in actual company situations, you should be thinking by now about the strategy of the organization you are managing or know best. Against the general need to articulate and appraise its strategy and with the aim of generating alternatives for its improvement, these questions should focus attention upon the usefulness to you of what you have just been reading.

What really is our product? What functions does it serve? To what additional functions might it be extended or adapted?

What is happening to the market for our products? Is it expanding or contracting? Why?

What are our company's major strengths and weaknesses? From what sources do these arise?

Do we have a distinctive or core competence? If so, to what new activities can it be applied?

What is the structure of our industry? Who are its leaders? What are its subgroups of companies? Where do we fit? How is the industry changing?

What are our principal competitors' major strengths and weaknesses? Are they imitating us or we them? What comparative advantage over our competitors can we exploit?

What is our strategy? Is the combination of product and market an optimum economic strategy? Is the central nature of our business clear enough to provide us with a criterion for product diversification?

What, if any, better combinations of market opportunities and distinctive competence can our company effect, within a range of reasonable risk?

These questions may prove helpful in the task of designing or validating an economic strategy. However, they are never wholly sufficient because the strategic decision is never wholly economic in character. Corporate strategy is much more than a series of product-market decisions.

Chapter 4

The Company and Its Strategists: Relating Corporate Strategy to Personal Values

Up to this point we have argued that a concept of purpose and a sense of direction strengthen a company's ability to survive in changing circumstances. We have seen the difficulties of understanding clearly both a company's circumstances and its strengths and weaknesses. The action implied by these difficulties is an objective and alert surveillance of the environment for threats and opportunities and a detached appraisal of organizational characteristics in order to identify distinctive competence. We have considered the suitable combination of a company's strengths and its opportunities to be a logical exercise characterized by perhaps not precise but reasoned, well-informed choices of alternatives assuring the highest possible profit. We have been examining the changing relationship of company and environment almost as if a purely economic strategy, uncontaminated by the personality or goals of the decision maker, were possible.

Strategy as Projection of Preference

We must acknowledge at this point that there is no way to divorce the decision determining the most sensible economic strategy for a company from the personal values of those who make the choice. Executives in charge of company destinies do not look exclusively at what a company might do and can do. In apparent disregard of the second of these considerations, they sometimes seem heavily influenced by what they personally *want* to do.

We are ourselves not aware of how much desire affects our own choice of alternatives, but we can see it in others. In the 1950s George Romney, then president of American Motors, began a dramatic promotion of economically sensible transportation that might have developed the market for small cars before the Japanese sensationally exploited that new segment. After the solvency of his company was assured, he repaid every dollar of debt owed by American Motors. If he had invested instead in the development of an efficient engine and in variations in the small car appealing to different market segments, he might have retained leadership in a sector of the market long ignored by his Big Three competitors.

Almost certainly we see reflected here the higher value Romney placed on economy than on consumer preferences, on liquidity over debt, and on other values derived more from his character and religious upbringing than from an objective monitoring of the best course for American Motors to follow. Romney's successors, with less distinctive personal values but just as subjective preferences, reverted to the General Motors big-car strategy. The latter gave way so belatedly to a visibly changing environment that the future of the U.S. auto industry, if unprotected from Japanese imports, remains in doubt.

Frank Farwell came from IBM to the presidency of Underwood in 1955, it has been reported in a classic anecdote, saying he would be damned if he would spend his life peddling adding machines and typewriters. This aversion may explain why Underwood plunged into the computer business without the technical, financial, or marketing resources necessary to succeed in it. Similarly, when Adriano Olivetti purchased control of Underwood after three days of hurried negotiations, he may well have been moved by his childhood memory of visiting Hartford, Connecticut, and by the respect for the world's once leading manufacturer of typewriters that led his father to erect in Ivrea a replica of the red-brick, five-story Hartford plant.[1] That he wanted to purchase Underwood so badly may explain why he and his associates did not find out how dangerously it had decayed and how near bankruptcy it had been brought.

The three presidents of J. I. Case between 1953 and 1963 seem to have been displaying their own temperaments as they wracked the company with alternating expansionism and contraction far

---

[1] See "Underwood-Olivetti (AR)," Edmund P. Learned, C. Roland Christensen, Kenneth R. Andrews, and William D. Guth, *Business Policy: Text and Cases,* original edition (Homewood, Ill.: Richard D. Irwin, Inc., 1965), p. 212. This case is also in the Intercollegiate Case Clearing House, (Boston, 02163) No. 9–312–017.

beyond the needs of response to a cyclical industry environment.[2] In all these cases, the actions taken can be rationalized so as not to seem quite so personal as I have suggested they are.

The Inevitability of Values

We will be able to understand the strategic decision better if we admit rather than resist the dimension of preference. We tell ourselves that our personal inclinations harmonize with the optimum combination of economic opportunity and company capability. Professional managers in a large company, drilled in analytical technique and the use of staff trained to subordinate value-laden assumptions to tables of numbers, may often actually prefer the optimal economic strategy because its suitability is strongly satisfying. Certain entrepreneurs, whose energy and personal drives far outweigh their formal training and self-awareness, set their course in directions not necessarily supported by logical appraisal. Such disparity appears most frequently in small privately held concerns or in companies built by successful and self-confident owner-managers. The phenomenon we are discussing, however, may appear in any company, especially if it is large, or in its divisions.

Our problem now can be very simply stated. In examining the alternatives available to a company, we must henceforth consider the preferences of the chief executive. Furthermore, we must also be concerned with the values of other key managers who must either contribute to or assent to the strategy if it is to be effective. Finally, at a higher level of sophistication, the strategy should have some appeal for all employees. Their opportunity for superior implementation can contribute, under receptive leadership, to improved productivity and continuous adaptation to customer needs. Bureaucratic constraints and autocratic, multilayered supervision often choke off the constructive by-products of the enthusiastic cooperation that convergence of individual and corporate goals produces.

We therefore have three levels of reconciliation to consider— first, the divergence between the chief executive's preference and the strategic choice that seems most economically defensible; second, the conflict among several sets of managerial personal values that must be reconciled not only with an economic strategy but also with each other; and third, the difference in motivation of

---

[2] "J. I. Case Company," Learned et al., *Business Policy,* pp. 82–102. This case is also in the Intercollegiate Case Clearing House, No. 9–309–270.

management and the work force that must be transcended by participation in and acceptance of at least the organization components of the strategy.

Thus, when Edgar Villchur, inventor of the acoustic suspension loudspeaker, founded Acoustic Research, Inc., in 1954, he institutionalized a desire to bring high fidelity sound to the mass market at the lowest possible cost. He licensed his competitors freely and finally gave up his original patent rights. He kept not only his prices but also his dealer margins low, maintained for a considerable time a primitive production facility and an organization of friends rather than managers, and went to great lengths to make the company a good place to work, sharing with employees the company's success. The company was dominated by Mr. Villchur's desire to have a small organization characterized by academic, scientific, and intellectual rather than "commercial" values. Product development was driven by some of these values away from the acoustical technology that Mr. Villchur's personal competence would have suggested into development of record players, amplifiers, and tuners that offered less superiority over competitive products than did his speakers. Again, these were priced far below what might have been possible.

Abraham Hoffman, for years vice president and treasurer, had the task of trying to overcome his superior's reluctance to advertise, to admit the validity of the marketing function, and to run the business as a profitable enterprise. That the company had succeeded in at long last developing and producing a music system of great value in relation to its cost and in winning the respect of the high fidelity listener market does not alter the fact that the first determination of strategy came more from Mr. Villchur's antibusiness values rather than from an analytical balancing of opportunity and distinctive competence. The latter would have led, with perhaps much greater growth and profitability, into acoustical systems, public address equipment, long-distance communications, hearing aids, noise suppression, and the like—all areas in which technical improvement in the quality of available sound is much needed.

We must remember, however, that it is out of Mr. Villchur's determination and goals that his company came into being in the first place. The extraordinary accomplishments of an antimarketing company in the marketplace are directly traceable to the determination to innovate in quality and price. The reconciliation between Mr. Villchur's values and Mr. Hoffman's more business-oriented determination to manage the company's growth more objectively occurred only when the company was sold to Teledyne, Inc., Mr. Villchur retired to his laboratory, and Mr. Hoffman became president. The quality achievements of this firm have been rewarded, but the economic potential of its strategy was for years underrealized.

We should admit that the personal desires, aspirations, and needs of the senior managers of a company *do* play an influential role in the determination of strategy. Against those who are offended by this idea either for its departure from the stereotype of single-minded economic man or for its implicit violation of responsibilities to the shareholder, we would argue that we must accept not only the inevitability but also the desirability of this intervention. If we begin by saying all strategic decisions must fall within the very broad limits of the manager's fiduciary responsibility to the owners of the business and perhaps to others in the management group, then we may proceed legitimately to the idea that what a manager wants to do is not out of order. The conflict that often arises between what general managers want to do and what the dictates of economic strategy suggest they ought to do is best not denied or condemned. It should be accepted as a matter of course. In the study of organization behavior, we have long since concluded that the personal needs of the hourly worker must be taken seriously and at least partially satisfied as a means of securing the productive effort for which wages are paid. It should, then, come as no surprise that the president of the corporation also arrives at his work with his own needs and values, to say nothing of his relatively greater power to see that they are taken into account.

Reconciling Divergent Values

If we accept the inevitability of personal values in the strategic decision governing the character and course of a corporation, then we must turn to the skills required to reconcile the optimal economic strategy with the personal preferences of the company executives. There is no reason why a better balance could not have been struck in Acoustic Research without sacrifice to the genius of the founder or the quality of life in his company. It is first necessary to penetrate conventional rationalization and reticence to determine what these preferences are. For without this revelation, strategic proposals stemming from different unstated values come into conflict. This conflict cannot be reconciled by talking in terms of environmental data and corporate resources. The hidden agenda of corporate policy debates makes them endless and explains why so many companies do not have explicit, forthright, and usefully focused strategies.

To many caught up in the unresolved strategic questions in their own organizations, it seems futile even to attempt to reconcile a strategic alternative dictated by personal preference with other alternatives oriented toward capitalizing on opportunity. In actuality, however, this additional complication poses fewer difficulties than at first appear. The analysis of opportunity and the appraisal of resources themselves often lead in different directions. To compose three, rather than two, divergent sets of considerations into a single pattern may increase the complexity of the task, but the integrating process is still the same. We can look for the dominant consideration and treat the others as constraints; we can probe the elements in conflict for the possibilities of reinterpretation or adjustment. We are not building a wall of irregular stone so much as balancing a mobile of elements, the motion of which is adjustable to the motion of the entire mobile.

As we have seen, external developments can be affected by company action and company resources, and internal competence can be developed. If worst comes to worst, it is better for a person to separate from a management whose values he or she does not share than to pretend agreement or to wonder why others think as they do. Howard Head, whose passionate dedication to the metal ski not only produced a most successful business but also delayed unnecessarily that business's entry into plastic skis, realistically retired from his later diversified business and sold his holdings. It is not necessary, however, for all members of management to think alike or to have the same personal values, so long as strategic decision is not delayed or rendered ineffective by these known and accepted differences. Large gains are possible simply by raising the strategic issues for discussion by top management, by admitting the legitimacy of different preferences, and by exploring how superficial or fundamental the differences are.

In the periodic review of strategy, it has become common practice to assign a senior executive the task of interviewing all key managers in a company. The purpose of such conversations is to elicit each person's version of the mission and character of the company and to uncover, rather than smooth over, significant positive and negative feelings about past strategic decisions and possible alternatives for the future. In sessions where strategic direction is to be discussed and at least tentatively decided, these differences are explored without criticism. The ideal outcome is resolution of the differences or discovery of alternatives that make original disagreement irrelevant. The minimum sought is an understanding of the impact upon future results of important reservations by persons who know at least that they have been heard before being outvoted or overpowered.

Such discussions thrive in a cooperative management group led by a chief executive who understands that leadership is not productively comprised of unilateral decisions that leave the leader either marching alone or trailed by uncommitted subordinates. Grudging followers would be more conscious of their subordinacy than of their opportunity to be creative in serving corporate purpose. When a change in strategy has been successfully negotiated in management and board discussions, collision between that outcome and the goals of the other members of the organization is almost inevitable. The subject of concern then becomes the culture of the organization rather than the personal preferences of individuals.

Every organization develops patterns of relationships, usually informal, in which the authority of persons, customs, and objectives is recognized and embodied in traditional ways of doing things. Individual preferences coalesce to establish certain values as dominant and others as optional.

Some organizations, like Lincoln Electric, which prizes individual achievement and rewards it handsomely, are spare, no-frills, and highly productive companies succeeding against higher-cost and lower-quality competition. Others, like Du Pont, become institutions in which research and development, safety, and corporate uniformity, for example, tend to homogenize scores of divisions in dozens of industries. This process makes them more culturally Du Pont than individually ready to succeed in the stringent rough and tumble of their own competitive environments.

In the implementation of strategic change, the interconnection of strategy and previously institutionalized values is crucial. To overlook it, under the outmoded assumption that authority and logical analysis are adequate to override attachments to values brought under attack, is a common but unnecessary mistake. A change in corporate direction and the energy and innovation required to make it successful usually call for a cultural adaptation that is better encouraged than forced.[3]

Modification of Values

The question whether values can actually be changed during the reconciliation process is somewhat less clear. A value is a view of

---

[3]See Jay W. Lorsch, "The Invisible Barrier to Strategic Change," *California Management Review* (Winter 1986), pp. 95 ff.

life and a judgment of what is desirable that is very much a part of a person's personality and a group's morale. From parents, teachers, and peers, we are told by psychologists, we acquire basic values, which change somewhat with acquired knowledge, analytical ability, and self-awareness, but remain a stable feature of personality. Nonetheless, the preference attached to goals in concrete circumstances is not beyond influence. The physicist who leaves the university to work in a profit-making company because of a combined fondness for his work and for material comfort may ask to continue to do pure rather than applied research, but he presumably does not want his company to go bankrupt. The conflict in values is to some degree negotiable, once the reluctance to expose hidden agendas is overcome. Retaining the value orientation of the scientist, the ambivalent physicist might assent to a strategic alternative stressing product development rather than original investigation, at least for a specified time until the attainment of adequate profit makes longer range research feasible.

The recent restructuring of American industry has forced drastic changes in the culture of organizations. Foreign competition has revealed that American wage rates are often uncompetitive in relation to productivity. The architects of hostile takeovers, looking to sell assets of target companies, identify and dispense with what they consider to be unproductive assets, divisions, jobs, and people. The staff sections of corporate headquarters, grown large in the attempt to give expert attention to everything that might well be done rather than must be done, have been slashed. Downsizing and consequent layoffs, painful as they are to contemplate, attract attention to the problem being addressed. Survivors, however demoralized, are energized by the struggle to survive and become aware of the need to develop new ways to get done what must be done. It is unfortunate in such instances that less drastic measures were not undertaken earlier. Strategic innovation is a practical alternative to violent restructuring.

Even so large a company as General Motors, not yet in deep trouble, is self-consciously restructuring itself in an industry changing in ways that make its previous organization structure, procurement, labor relations, and production methods obsolete. Du Pont is attempting to define its mission, adapt its culture-shaping policies to the conditions of the industries in which it participates, and differentiate its management style to suit the needs of subsidiaries. The merger of a large international oil company with its oil field and market cultural characteristics has dramatized the decorum and stability of Du Pont. General Electric has recently radically reduced its corporate staff and assigned responsibility to its divisions to succeed on their own against their competitors rather than to view themselves as under the protection of the corporate monogram. A new kind of giant corporation is in the making.

That under adversity the culture of an organization and the values of its leaders can change has been recently established beyond doubt. Units divested dramatically from their corporate parents have often become more profitable and pleasant to work in as the burden of corporate allocations and compliance with corporate policy has been lifted. The opportunity wasted by our basic industries is that presented by this book. The conditions confronting the automobile, steel, chemical, textile, and footwear industries have been visible for years. The failure to adapt to change that had become clearly inevitable reflects the triumph of habit and short-term measurement of results over strategic assessment of company position in a changing world. The faltering of American industry, affected to be sure by forces other than managerial ineptness, is a dramatic background to the need to devise a strategy against a conservative culture suppressing innovation and adaptation.

Awareness of Values

Our interest in the role of personal values in strategic formulations should not be confined to assessing the influence of other people's values. Despite the well-known problems of introspection, we can probably do more to understand the relation of our own values to our choice of purpose than we can to change the values of others. Awareness that our own preference for an alternative opposed by another stems from values as much as from rational estimates of economic opportunity may have important consequences. First, it may make us more tolerant and less indignant when we perceive this relationship between recommendations and values in the formulations of others. Second, it will force us to consider how important it really is to us to maintain a particular value in making a particular decision. Third, it may give us insight with which to identify our biases and pave the way for a more objective assessment of all the strategic alternatives that are available. These consequences of self-examination will not end conflict, but they will at least prevent its unnecessary prolongation.

The object of this self-examination is not necessarily to endow us with the ability to persuade others to accept the strategic recommendations we consider best: it is to acquire insight into the problems of determining purpose and skill in the process of resolving those problems. Individuals inquiring into their own values for the purpose of understanding their own positions in policy debates can continue to assess their own personal opportunities, strengths and weaknesses, and basic values by means of the procedures outlined here. A personal strategy, analytically considered and consciously developed, may be as useful to an individual as a corporate strategy is to a business institution. The effort to formulate personal purpose might well accompany each individual's contributions to organizational purpose. If the encounter leads to a clarification of the purposes one seeks, the values one holds, and the alternatives available, the attempt to make personal use of the concept of strategy will prove extremely worthwhile.

Introducing personal preference forces us to deal with the possibility that the strategic decision we prefer (identified after the most nearly objective analysis of opportunity and resources we are capable of) is not acceptable to other executives with different values. Their acceptance of the strategy is necessary to its successful implementation. In diagnosing this conflict, we try to identify the values implicit in our own choice. As we look at the gap between the strategy that follows from our own values and the strategy that would be appropriate to the values of our associates, we look to see whether the difference is fundamental or superficial. Then we look to see how the strategy we believe best matches opportunity and resources can be adapted to accommodate the values of those who will implement it. Reconciliation of the three principal determinants of strategy that we have so far considered is often made possible by adjustment of any or all of the determinants.

The role of self-examination in coming to terms with a conflict in values over an important strategic determination is not to turn all strategic decisions into outcomes of consensus. Some organizations are run by persons who are leaders in the sense that they have power and are not afraid to use it. It is true that business leaders, in Zaleznik's words, "commit themselves to a career in which they have to work on themselves as a condition for effective working and working with other people."[4] At the same time, a leader must recognize that "the essence of leadership is choice, a singularly individualistic act in which a [person] assumes respon-

---

[4] Abraham Zaleznik and Manfred F. R. Kets de Vries, *Power and the Corporate Mind* (Boston: Houghton Mifflin, 1975), p. 207.

sibility for a commitment to direct an organization along a particular path.... As much as a leader wishes to trust others, he has to judge the soundness and validity of his subordinates' positions. Otherwise, the leader may become a prisoner of the emotional commitments of his subordinates, frequently at the expense of making correct judgments about policies and strategies."[5]

When a management group is locked in disagreement, the presence of power and the need for its exercise condition the dialogue. There are circumstances when the exercise of leadership must transcend disagreement that cannot be resolved by discussion. Subordinates, making the best of the inevitable, must accept a follower role. When leadership becomes irresponsible and dominates subordinate participation without reason, it is usually ineffective or is deposed. Participants in strategic disagreements must know not only their own needs and power but also those of the chief executive. Strategic management, in the sense that power attached to value plays a role in it, is a political process.

You should obviously not warp your recommended strategy to the detriment of your company's future in order to adjust it to the personal values you hold or observe. On the other hand, you should not expect to be able to impose without risk and without expectation of eventual vindication and agreement, an unwelcome pattern of purposes and policies on the people in charge of a corporation or responsible for achieving results. Strategy is a human construction; it must in the long run be responsive to human needs. It must ultimately inspire commitment. It must stir an organization to successful striving against competition. People have to have their hearts in it.

---

[5]Ibid., p. 209.

Chapter 5

The Company and Its Responsibilities to Society: Relating Corporate Strategy to Ethical Values

We come at last to the fourth component of strategy formulation—the moral and social implications of what once was considered a purely economic choice. In our consideration of strategic alternatives, we have come from what strategists *might* and *can* do to what they *want* to do. We now move to what they *ought* to do—from the viewpoint of various leaders and segments of society and their own standards of right and wrong.

Ethical behavior, like the exercise of preference, may be considered a product of values. To some the suggestion that an orderly and analytical process of strategy determination should include the discussion of highly controversial ethical issues, about which honest differences of opinion are common and self-deceiving rationalization endless, is repugnant. The mid-1980s have witnessed a wave of corporate wrongdoing, however, that is impossible to ignore. It recalls the post-Watergate days during which more than 300 companies turned themselves in to the Securities and Exchange Commission (SEC). Their confessions included illegal political contributions, questionable payments to overseas agents and customers, outright bribes, and improper accounting practices. The dismissal of the top leadership of such respected corporations as Gulf Oil and Lockheed could not compare to the forced resignations of a vice president and president of the United States, but in the eyes of the public the belief that business people and politicians were equally corrupt was reinforced.

The misdemeanors of the majority of the companies reporting to the SEC were most notable for having been discovered by the companies themselves and voluntarily disclosed, albeit as an alternative to risking the harsher penalties that might have resulted from formal investigations. It was reassuring to know how minor but disturbing to see how routine most of the transgressions turned out to be. Most of them had apparently occurred without the knowledge of top managements, which had issued policies excluding such practices. This circumstance was heartening to those who wished to think that corporate leadership was honest, but disheartening to those disappointed to find leaders gullible or inept in enforcing ethical policy adopted for important reasons.

Public Opinion of Managerial Malfeasance

Just as the humiliation of the Vietnam War and Watergate was being forgotten, the resurgence of media attention to illegal, unethical, or generally questionable activities refueled the opinion polls that once again regularly reported that a majority of the respondents thought business people generally dishonest. Defense contractors like General Dynamics Corporation and General Electric were found to have overcharged the government even to the extent of forging time cards. Ostensibly outrageous charges for spare parts made the $600 toilet seat a symbol of corporate greed without consideration of the complex specifications or defective procurement procedures that were proffered as explanations.

The Johns-Manville Corporation was charged with concealing for years its knowledge that asbestos caused long delayed and ultimately fatal disease. The makers of the Dalkon Shield, an intrauterine contraceptive device, caused wonderment that such people of the philanthropic generosity, cultivation, and background as those owning and running the company could have first not known and then not heeded the impact of its product. The chief executive officer of the Bank of Boston asserted that if he knew of the law that cash transactions of more than $10,000 should be reported to the Internal Revenue Service for the purpose of inquiring into the laundering of money he had no way of knowing the regulation was not being complied with. That paper bags full of cash deposited by suspected Mafia chieftains went unreported by a branch manager was a dramatic indication either of deliberate violation of the law or of an almost incredible failure to make it known. It was almost immediately revealed that many banks throughout the United States have not complied with a law that was hardly a secret.

In another area of management malfeasance, perhaps unknown to top managers, the Exxon Corporation was forced early in 1986 to pay a multibillion-dollar fine to the states as compensation for oil overcharges during the time of differential price controls for domestic and imported product. E. F. Hutton was wracked first by the discovery that some of its branch managers engaged in 2,000 instances of overdrafting to achieve, in effect, interest-free loans and then by the revelation that other irregularities symptomatic of ethically deficient individual behavior and malfunctioning incentive systems had occurred. Even the friendliest observers of business activity could not help wondering how much more of an iceberg of illegality and administrative ineptness was awaiting discovery.

That a few of our venerable corporate institutions are tarnished by scandal could not shake public confidence in business as a whole except for one easily misinterpreted fact. No business leaders of the stature that commands media attention criticized this wrongdoing or distanced themselves openly from the decisions and behavior of the few, though conspicuous, offenders. Their silence can be understood. It is not becoming for corporate CEOs to denounce their acquaintances or friends (except when hostile takeovers make them enemies), especially because they see others and themselves vulnerable to betrayal by their own organizations. They are aware of how difficult it is to draw the line under stringent competition between aggressive and unethical behavior. The imperfection of control and audit systems makes it impossible to detect every instance of deliberate and clever fraud, to say nothing of creeping erosion of moral standards in small matters. The decentralization of authority that makes large organizations possible requires trust rather than suspicion in the granting of appropriate autonomy to subordinates. Human weakness and organization fallibility make it imprudent for executives to be self-righteous in their criticism of business practice.

The silence of business leaders, however understandable, unmistakably communicates tolerance of flagrant misbehavior. It suggests complicity to the watching public, unaware of the complexity of enforcing ethical policy and compliance throughout a large organization or the undesirability of limiting the latitude to do the wrong thing by imitating the controls of a police state. The general conclusion that business is dishonest and immoral is a high price to pay for lack of competence in how to include high standards of conduct in the strategy of a company and make them effective through the same means used to decide, make known, and enforce policy in other matters.

The Inherently Amoral Corporation

Before we examine the proposition that the choice and pursuit of purpose are in part the product of moral judgments, we should consider a most important characteristic of corporate life that works against articulating and enforcing ethical policy. The legal and economic definition of the purpose of a corporation as maximum enhancement of shareholder wealth leads, however circuitously, to conclusions that behavior not blatantly illegal or immoral is quite acceptable—in fact required for success in competition.

Some observers, usually not wholehearted subscribers to what economists have made of the pronouncements of the moral philosopher Adam Smith, ask whether the profit maximization model of the corporation is not incomplete, obsolescent, and unreal. It is at least not a reliable guide to ethical behavior, which if achieved against the economic gains of being unethical usually carries a hefty monetary price.

The definition of the corporation as serving only the financial interests of the shareholders naturally leads to subordination of ethical concern to financial outcome. But apart from this historic miscommunication, other conditions of corporate life, unchecked by a comprehensive strategy, tend to make the corporation inherently amoral. These include the need to succeed felt by ambitious and energetic people, the wish to win that is integral to competition, the temptation to forsake the high road for shortcuts, and the pressure on people to achieve their plan and avoid penalty at substantial cost to community responsibility and ethical practice.

Pursuit of what you find correct in these statements may lead you to conclude that the modern, large, publicly held corporation needs a new theory and a new legal definition to legitimize its acknowledgment of responsibility, not only to its shareholders but also to its own membership, its customers, and its communities. The established corporation has become an institution in society governed by moral as well as economic values. Its strategists need moral as well as economic motives and competence. The corporate strategy governing their approach to future success in competition includes combining personal and moral aspirations with the choice of products and services to be provided to markets at levels of quality and value that reflect both ethical and economic intent.

For all these reasons, it is no longer possible to avoid discussing ethical issues. The discomfort and disagreement that complicate conversations in business are only a small investment in the valuable ability to recognize ethical dilemmas in advance of disaster and to avoid the kind of scandal that ruins careers and exacerbates public criticism of business.

The Moral Component of Corporate Strategy

The emerging view in the liberal-professional leadership of our most prominent corporations is that determining future strategy must take into account—as part of its social environment—steadily rising moral and ethical standards. Reconciling the conflict in responsibility that occurs when maximum profit and social contribution appear on the same agenda adds to the complexity of strategy formulation and its already clear demands for creativity. Coming to terms with the morality of choice may be the most strenuous undertaking in strategic decision.

Discussions of the responsibility of business have usually until now taken individual personal integrity for granted or have assumed that the courts were adequate discipline to ensure compliance with the law. The obvious necessity for explicit company policy now makes it necessary for decision to be made about at least how compliance with the law can be ensured. The first step is a stated policy that illegality will not be condoned and enforcement provisions will begin with corporate action rather than waiting for the law and the courts. Thus, corporate strategy now must extend beyond the implicit or explicit intention to be law abiding to policy designed to cope with the organization problems making obedience to the law difficult to achieve.

Because political contributions and bribery are neither illegal nor even unusual in other parts of the world, explicit policy must be made with respect to other marginal, technically legal, but in American eyes, improper kinds of payments. The Foreign Corrupt Practices Act deals with the difference between American and foreign law and custom. It includes a requirement that a company report its confidence in the adequacy of its control systems. Once embarked on this sea of uncertainty, companies are forced to include policy decisions about other corporate and personal behavior.

In most reputable companies it has long been assumed that economic objectives would be pursued within the law and the bounds of ethical custom. The current necessity to articulate and enforce an unspoken assumption leads to detailed consideration of the ethical quality of an organization's culture and to decisions governed by noneconomic criteria. Specifying and securing ethical behavior is so difficult in a large company in which responsibility is delegated through many levels of authority and degrees of autonomy, that the first step is to break the custom of silence to make possible the assertion of ethical concern.[1]

The Social Responsibility of Business

The morality of personal behavior, however, is not our only concern. The dominant position of the corporation in our society, the influence it has on all citizens, and its inevitable relations with local, state, and national governments make it increasingly important to consider, company by company, what the corporation's social responsibility will be. Milton Friedman still argues that the only social responsibility of business is to pursue profit as vigorously as possible (within the law and an undefined "ethical custom").[2] For a number of reasons, it is no longer possible to conclude that consideration of strategic alternatives should be any more free of concern for the impact of economic activity upon society than for the pressure toward unethical behavior it may exert on the members of the corporation.

First, corporate executives of the caliber, integrity, intelligence, and humanity capable of coping with the problems of personal morality just cited are not happy to be tarred with the brush of bribery and corruption. They are not likely to turn their backs on other problems involving corporate behavior. The recurring energy crises, the growing sensitivity to environmental damage by industrial and community operations, the protection of the consumer from intended or unwitting exploitation or deception, the extension of social justice as exemplified by the demands of minority populations and women for opportunity and recognition, the general concern for the limits of growth and the so-called quality of life—all these cannot be ignored. The need to respond as a matter of conscience as well as a matter of law is widely acknowledged.

Second, it is increasingly clear that government regulation is not a good substitute for knowledgeable self-restraint. As expectations for the protection and well-being of the environment, of customers, and of employees grow more insistent, it is clear that if

---

[1]For useful notes on ethical analysis in the practice of general management and an excellent bibliography of writings in the field, see John B. Matthews, Kenneth E. Goodpaster, and Laura L. Nash, *Policies and Persons: A Casebook in Business Ethics* (New York: McGraw-Hill Book Co., 1985).

[2]The classic statement of this position is still Friedman's *Capitalism and Freedom* (Chicago: The University of Chicago Press, 1962).

corporate power is to be regulated more by public law than by private conscience, much of our national energy will have to be spent keeping watch over corporate behavior, ferreting out problems, designing and revising detailed laws to deal with them, and enforcing these laws even as they become obsolete.

Executives assuming top management responsibility today may be more sensitive on the average than their predecessors to the upgrading of our goals as a society and more responsive to the opportunity to relate corporate and public purposes. But if not, they can be sure that new regulation will force this concern upon their strategic processes. Extending the reach of strategic decision to encompass public concerns is either a voluntary response permitting latitude in choice or acquiescence to law that may involve none. New forms of regulation or effective enforcement come late to the problem without regard for feasibility or cost. The strategist can consider much earlier whether the problem is susceptible to effective and economically satisfactory solution.

Categories of Concern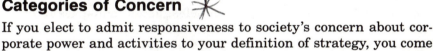

If you elect to admit responsiveness to society's concern about corporate power and activities to your definition of strategy, you come face to face with two major questions. What is the range of corporate involvement available to a company? What considerations should guide its choice of opportunity?

The World. The problems affecting the quality of life in the society to which the company belongs may usefully be thought of as extending through a set of densely populated spheres from the firm itself to the world community. The multinational firm, to take world society first, would find (within its economic contribution to industrialization in the developing countries) the need to measure what it takes out before it could judge its participation responsible. The willingness to undertake joint ventures rather than insist on full ownership, to share management and profits in terms not immediately related to the actual contributions of other partners, to cooperate otherwise with governments looking for alternatives to capitalism, to train nationals for skilled jobs and management positions, to reconcile different codes of ethical practice in matters of taxes and bribery—all illustrate the opportunity for combining entrepreneurship with responsibility and the terms in which strategy might be expressed. Even small firms now face the opportunity and necessity to export. In smaller ways they also must negotiate with host countries and pursue their self-interest in an environment of give and take.

The Nation. Within the United States, for a firm of national scope, problems susceptible to constructive attention from business occur in virtually every walk of life. To narrow a wide choice, a company would most naturally begin with the environmental consequences of its manufacturing processes or the impact of its products upon the public. Presumably a company would first put its own house in order or embark upon a long program to make it so. Then it might take interest in other problems, either through tax-deductible philanthropic contributions or through business ventures seeking economic opportunity in social need—for example, trash disposal or health care. Education, the arts, race relations, equal opportunity for women, or even such large issues as the impact upon society of technological change compete for attention.

The proper role of government in providing support for American industry now under attack by foreign competitors is of immediate concern to business leaders. In beleaguered industries like textiles, they must weigh the short-term advantages of protectionism versus the long-term superiority of free trade. Through organizations like the Business Roundtable, the American Business Conference, and the National Manufacturers Association, business leaders find themselves making recommendations to the executive branch and the Congress that must address public as well as corporate interest. Our agenda of national problems is extensive. It is not hard to find opportunities for constructive contribution. The question, as in product-market possibilities, is which ones to choose to work on.

Of even more practical concern, strategy must often be negotiated with government, as in the case of the automobile industry. Safety standards, fuel economy, pollution control, and import quotas require knowledge of public policy and regulatory agency strategy. Governments everywhere are active claimants to a voice in individual corporate strategy. The essential differences between private-sector management and public administration must be understood to be dealt with.[3]

The Local Community. Closer home are the problems of the communities in which the company operates. These constitute the

---

[3]See Joseph L. Bower, *The Two Faces of Management* (Boston: Houghton Mifflin, 1983).

urban manifestations of the national problems already referred to—inadequate housing, unemployment in the poverty culture, substandard medical care, and the like. The city, special focus of national decay and vulnerable to fiscal and other mismanagement, is an attractive object of social strategy because of its nearness and compactness. The near community allows the development of mutually beneficial corporate projects such as vocational training. Business cannot remain healthy in a sick community.

The Industry. Moving from world to country to city takes us through the range of social and political issues that engage the attention of corporate strategists who wish to factor social responsibility into their planning. Two other less obvious but even more relevant avenues of action should be considered—the industry or industries in which the company operates and the quality of life within the company itself. Every industry, like every profession, has problems that arise from a legacy of indifference, stresses of competition, and the real or imagined impossibility of interfirm cooperation under the antitrust laws. Every industry has chronic problems of its own, such as safety, product quality, pricing, and pollution, in which only cooperative action can effectively pick up where regulation leaves off or makes further regulation unnecessary.

The Company. Within the firm itself, a company has open opportunities for satisfying its aspirations to responsibility. The quality of any company's present strategy, for example, is probably always subject to improvement, as new technology and higher aspirations work together. But besides such important tangible matters as the quality of goods and services being offered to the public and the maintenance and improvement of craftsmanship, there are three other areas which in the future will become much more important than they seem now. The first of these is the review process set up to estimate the quality of top-management decision. The second is the impact upon individuals of the control systems and other organization processes installed to secure results. The third is a recognition of the role of the individual in the corporation.

Review of Management Concerns for Responsibility

The everyday pressures bearing on decisions about what to do and how to get it done make almost impossible the kind of detached self-criticism essential to the perpetuation of responsible freedom. The opportunity to provide for systematic review sessions becomes more explicit and self-conscious. At any rate, as a category of concern, how a management can maintain sufficient detachment to estimate without self-deception the quality of its management performance is as important as any other. The proper role of the board of directors in performing this function—long ago lost sight of—is undergoing revitalization.

The caliber and strategic usefulness of a board of directors will nonetheless remain the option of the chief executives, who usually determine its function. How much they use their boards for improving the quality of corporate strategy and planning turns, as usual, on the sincerity of their interest and skill. Recent research has illuminated the irresponsibility of inaction in the face of problems requiring the perspective available only to properly constituted boards. This organization resource is available to general managers who recognize dormancy as waste and seek counsel in cases of conflicting responsibility. A number of large corporations, including General Motors, have established Public Responsibility Committees of the board to focus attention on social issues.

The effective provision by a board of responsible surveillance of the moral quality of a management's strategic decisions means that recent stirrings of concern about conflicts of interest will soon result in the withdrawal from boards of bankers representing institutions performing services to the company, of lawyers (in some instances) representing a firm retained by the company, and other suppliers or customers, as well as more scrupulous attention to present regulations about interlocking interests. As much attention is now given to avoiding the possibility of imputing conflict of interest to a director as to avoiding the actual occurrence. Stronger restrictions on conflict of interest will also affect employees of the firm, including the involvement of individuals with social-action organizations attacking the firm.

Impact of Control Systems on Ethical Performance

The ethical and economic quality of an organization's performance is vitally affected by its control system, which inevitably leads people, if it is effective at all, to do what will make them look good in the terms of the system rather than what their opportunities and problems, which the system may not take cognizance of, actually require. We will examine the unintended consequences of control and measurements systems when we come to the implementation of corporate strategy. In the meantime we should note that unanticipated pressures to act irresponsibly may be applied by top management who would deplore this consequence if they knew of it. The process of promotion, by which persons are moved from place to place so fast they do not develop concern for the problems of the community in which they live or effective relationships within which to accomplish anything, unintentionally weakens the participation of executives in community affairs. The tendency to measure executives in divisionalized companies on this year's profits reduces sharply their motivation to invest in social action with returns over longer times. Lifelong habits of neutrality and noninvolvement eventually deprive the community, in a subtle weakening of its human resources, of executive experience and judgment. Executive cadres are in turn deprived of real-life experience with political and social systems they ultimately need.

The Individual and the Corporation

The actual quality of life in a business organization turns most crucially on how much freedom is accorded to the individual. Most firms consider responsibility to their members as important as external constituencies. It is as much a matter of enlightened self-interest as of responsibility to provide conditions encouraging the convergence of the individual's aspirations with those of the corporation, to provide conditions for effective productivity, and to reward employees for extraordinary performance.

   With the entry of the corporation into controversial areas comes greater interest on the part of organization members to take part in public debate. It becomes possible for individuals to make comments on social problems that could be embarrassing to the corporation. It is at best difficult to balance the freedom of individuals and the consequences of their participation in public affairs against the interests of the corporation. The difficulty is increased if the attitudes of management, which are instinctively overprotective of the corporation, are harsh and restrictive. Short-run embarrassments and limited criticism from offended groups—even perhaps a threatened boycott—may be a small price to pay for the continued productivity within the corporation of people whose interests are deep and broad enough to cause them to take stands on public issues. The degree to which an organization is efficient, productive, creative, and capable of development is dependent in large part on the maintenance of a climate in which the individual does not feel suppressed and in which a kind of freedom (analogous to that the corporation enjoys in a free enterprise society) is permitted as a matter of course. Overregulation of the individual by corporate policy is no more appropriate than overregulation of the corporation by government. On the other hand, personal responsibility is as appropriate to individual liberty as corporate responsibility is to corporate freedom.

The Range of Concerns

What corporate strategists have to be concerned with, then, ranges from the most global of the problems of world society to the uses of freedom by a single person in the firm. The problems of their country, community, and industry lying between these extremes make opportunity for social contribution exactly coextensive with the range of economic opportunity before them. The problem of choice may be met in the area of responsibility in much the same way as in product-market combinations and in developing a program for growth and diversification.

The business firm, as an organic entity intricately affected by and affecting its environment, is as appropriately adaptive, our concept of corporate strategy suggests, to demands for responsible behavior as for economic service. Special satisfactions and prestige, if not economic rewards, are available for companies that are not merely adaptive but take the lead in shaping the moral and ethical environment within which their primary economic function is performed. Such firms are more persuasive than others, moreover, in convincing the public of the inherent impossibility of satisfying completely all the conflicting claims made upon business.

Choice of Strategic Alternatives for Social Action

The choice of avenues in which to participate will, of course, be influenced by the personal values of the managers making the decision. In the absence of powerful predispositions, the inner coherence of the corporate strategy would be extended by choosing issues most closely related to the economic strategy of the company, to the expansion of its markets, to the health of its immediate environment, and to its own industry and internal problems. The extent of appropriate involvement depends importantly on the resources available. Because the competence of the average corporation outside its economic functions is severely limited, it follows that a company should not venture into good works that are not strategically related to its present and prospective economic functions.

As in the case of personal values and individual idiosyncrasy, a company may be found making decisions erratically related to nonstrategic motives. However noble these may be, they are not made strategic and thus defensible and valid by good intentions alone. Rather than make large contributions to X University because its president is an alumnus, the company might better develop a pattern of educational support that blends its involvement in the whole educational system, its acknowledged debt for the contributions of technical or managerial education to the company, and its other contributions to its communities. What makes participation in public affairs strategic rather than improvisatory is (as we have seen in conceiving economic strategy) a definition of objectives taking all other objectives into account and a plan that reflects the company's definition of itself not only as a purveyor of goods and services but also as a responsible institution in its society.

The strategically directed company then will have a strategy for support of community institutions as explicit as its economic strategy and as its decisions about the kind of organization it intends to be and the kind of people it intends to attract to its membership. It is easy and proper, when margins allow it, to make full use of tax deductibility through contributions, from which the company expects no direct return. The choice of worthy causes, however, should relate to the company's concept of itself and thus directly to its economic mission. It should enter into new social service fields with the same questions about its resources and competence that new product-market combinations inspire. In good works as in new markets, opportunity without the competence to develop it is illusory. Deliberate concentration on limited objectives is preferable to scattered short-lived enthusiasm across a community's total need.

Policy for ethical and moral personal behavior, once the level of integrity has been decided, is not complicated by a wide range of choice. The nature of the company's operations defines the areas of vulnerability—purchasing, rebates, price fixing, fee splitting, customs facilitation, bribery, dubious agents' fees, conflict of interest, theft, or falsification of records. Where problems appear or danger is sensed, specific rules can be issued. As in the case of government regulation of the firm, these should not be overdetailed or mechanical, for there is no hope of anticipating the ingenuity of the willful evader. Uncompromising penalties for violations of policy intent or the rarely specified rule will do more to clarify strategy in this area than thousands of words beforehand. The complexity of elevating individual behavior is thus a matter of implementation of strategy more properly discussed in the context of organization processes such as motivation and control.

Determination of Strategy

We have now before us the major determinants of strategy. The principal aspects of formulation are (1) appraisal of present and foreseeable opportunity and risk in the company's environment, (2) assessment of the firm's unique combination of present and potential corporate resources or competences, (3) determination of the noneconomic personal and organizational preferences to be satisfied, and (4) identification and acceptance of the social responsibilities of the firm. The strategic decision is one that can be reached only after all these factors have been considered and the implications of each assessed.

In your efforts to analyze the situation of your own organization, you have experienced much more of the problem of the strategist than can be described on paper. When you have relinquished your original idea as to what a company's strategy should be in favor of a more imaginative one, you have seen that the formulation process has an essential creative and entrepreneurial aspect. In your effort to differentiate your thinking about your company from the conventional thinking of its industry, you may have become alert to new opportunities and new applications of corporate competence. You may still find it strange to define a product in terms of its present and potential functions rather than of its physical properties. You have probably made a start on how to assess the special competence of your firm from its past accomplishments and how to identify values and aspirations. You may have tried to rank preferences in order of their strength—your own among others.

The problem implicit in striking a balance between the company's apparent opportunity and its evident competence, between your own personal values and concepts of responsibility and those of the company's other members, is not an easy one. The concepts we have been discussing should help you make a decision, but they will not determine your decision for you. Whenever choice is compounded of rational analysis that can have more than one outcome, of aspiration and desire that can run the range of human ambition, and a sense of responsibility that changes the appeal of alternatives, it cannot be reduced to quantitative approaches or to the exactness management science can apply to narrower questions. Managers contemplating strategic decisions must be willing to make them without the guidance of decision rules, with confidence in their own judgment, which will have been seasoned by repeated analyses of similar questions. They must be aware more than one decision is possible and they are not seeking the single right answer. They can take encouragement from the fact that the manner in which an organization implements the chosen program can help to validate the original decision.

Some of the most difficult choices confronting a company are those that must be made among several alternatives that appear equally attractive and desirable. Once the analysis of opportunity has produced an inconveniently large number of possibilities, any firm has difficulty deciding what it wants to do and how the new activities will be related to the old.

In situations where opportunity is approximately equal and economic promise is offered by a range of activities, the problem of making a choice can be reduced by reference to the essential character of the company and to the kind of company the executives wish to run. The study of alternatives from this point of view will sooner or later reveal the greater attractiveness of some choices over others. Economic analysis and calculations of return on investment, though of course essential, may not crucially determine the outcome. Rather, the logjam of decision can be broken only by a frank exploration of executive aspirations regarding future development, including perhaps the president's own wishes with respect to the kind of institution he or she prefers to head, carried on as part of a free and untrammeled investigation of what human needs the organization would find satisfaction in serving. That return on investment alone will point the way ignores the values implicit in the calculations and the contribution an enthusiastic commitment to new projects can make. The rational examination of alternatives and the determination of purpose are among the most important and most neglected of all human activities. The final decision, which should be made as deliberately as possible after a detailed consideration of the issues we have attempted to separate, is an act of will and desire as much as of intellect.

Chapter 6

The Implementation of Strategy: Achieving Commitment to Purpose

We now turn our attention to attitudes and skills essential to the accomplishment of purpose. An idea is not complete or even completely understood until it is put into action. A unique corporate strategy is only rhetoric until it is embodied in organization activities that are guided by the strategy but in turn continually reshape it. Goal-directed implementation, the essence of strategic management, is far more complex than the execution of directions implied in the classic model of the hierarchical corporation.

The determination of strategy, as we have said before, can be thought of as a combination of four primarily analytical subactivities: examination of the company's environment for opportunity and risk, careful assessment of corporate strengths and weaknesses, identification and weighing of personal values built into the character of the company and its leaders, and establishment of the level of ethical and social responsibility to which it will hold itself.

The implementation of strategy may also be thought of as having essential subactivities. On the action side of corporate strategy these are primarily administrative rather than analytical in nature. Administrative action involves relationships among people, achievement and acceptance of authority, and much else, like energy or morality, that is not the product of mind alone. Implementation consists most broadly of achieving and sustaining commitment to purpose. Secondly, implementation is directed toward organized achievement of results through three universal structural processes: the specialization of task responsibilities, the coordination of divided responsibility, and the provision of a system of information enabling specialists and general managers alike to know what they need to know to act strategically. Each of these processes tends to develop counterstrategically by elevating its own special purposes above the needs of the total company.

Thirdly, the essential balance between individual and organization needs is sought through four familiar processes: measurement of performance, provision of incentives and rewards, establishment of constraints and controls, and recruitment and development of persons for operating and managing positions. These processes also tend to seek out their own separate purposes; they must be reined in and harnessed to corporate goals.

Finally, the role of leadership throughout the company in the accomplishment, modification, and extension of purpose in the innovative and adaptive corporation becomes more crucial as participation in strategy formulation becomes more extensive. We will come to see corporate strategy as, in part, the evolving product of commitment, vindicating and adapting to reality its initial formulation. We will see it also as the key to simplicity, economy, and superiority in the management of what would otherwise be confusing and needlessly complex affairs.

Distorted Approaches to Implementation

In part, because of the neglect of implementation as integral to strategy, the concept has been battered by distortion over the past 20 years. False hope, oversimplification, and naiveté, as well as zest for power, have often led, for example, to the assumption that the chief executive officer conceives strategy single-mindedly, talks the board of directors into pro forma approval, announces it as fixed policy, and expects it to be promptly executed by subordinates under conventional command and control procedures. This unilateral dominance is often at least partly feasible in the entrepreneurial startup stage, but when the company grows to something other than a one-person show, it becomes a political and social entity. When an established corporation is long dominated by strategic dictatorship, both outspoken and covert resistance eventually limits achievement.

The belief that strategy formulation, under the name of strategic planning, is primarily a staff activity, assisted by consulting firms, is a related distortion made possible by ignoring the problems of implementation. The assumption that strategy is essentially a value-free appraisal and choice of economic opportunity and evaluation of results without reference to company capability, personal values, and entrenched cultural loyalties has often led to strategic recommendations by staff departments and consulting firms that companies were neither able nor willing to carry out. Many planning techniques, useful in limited application, developed as quick-fix solutions to the need for better performance in competition.

Goals often tended to be expressed in terms of high growth rates in sales and profits, mindlessly compounded over future years. Economic objectives were chosen more for their theoretical growth potential than for company capability to attain them. Acquisitions were pursued for the sake of growth in the 1970s, just as hostile takeovers are undertaken in the 1980s in pursuit of financial strategies largely unrelated to the distinctive competence to make them work. In fact, financial strategies that follow a modern finance theory divorced from the concept of corporate strategy focus on the acquisition and divestment of assets, the extension of leverage to its limits without reference to impact on human resources, future development, and the capacity to service enormous debt should economic adversity put pressure on the company.

The catalogue of strategic mismanagement made possible by ignoring the human, social, and ethical elements in the pattern of corporate purpose would make dreary reading if it were ever to be compiled. Even without it, poor performance in the marketplace has exposed overrated techniques and fashionable shortcuts. The backlash against strategic planning occurring in the 1980s is largely justified and wholly understandable, but it has produced its own distortions. It has led to sweeping criticisms of American management and business education. Extreme incrementalism, understood as reactive improvisation, muddling through, or following one's nose, has been disinterred from the conceptual graveyard to justify avoidance of all forms of conscious planning.[1]

The venerable antistrategic position that organizations cannot have purposes as distinct from the special interests of individuals forming coalitions of rival aspirations is revived by disillusion with formal planning techniques. These prove defective when misapplied so as to elevate quantitative analysis over qualitative appraisal of the needs of an organization viewed as a whole. Other process distortions lead to finessing strategic decision by inspiring the entire organization with folkloric simplicities like "being close

---

[1]This position is not to be confused with the purposeful incrementalism recommended in James Brian Quinn's *Strategies for Change: Logical Incrementalism* (Homewood, Ill.: Richard D. Irwin, Inc., 1980).

to the customer," "managing by walking around," and "fostering continuous innovation." These phrases are attractive vacuities. What direction leadership should take, and what its content should consist of, is missing from these prescriptions. An implicit or explicit strategy is required to encourage something to *happen* in the close relationship to customers, to identify *what* managers should have in mind when they walk around, and to suggest constructive *direction* and *completion* of innovation.

Flexibility in Pursuit of Purpose

Intelligent implementation of the more comprehensive and substantive strategy proposed here presumes a balance between focus and flexibility, between a sense of direction and responsiveness to changing opportunities. It is true that announcing very specific and restrictive objectives can bar participation. Overly specific targets can lead to centralized decision making, politicized opposition, and rigidity.[2] Such goals should neither be adopted nor announced. Corporate strategy need not be a straitjacket. Room for variation, extension, and innovation must be provided. General goals, like the intention to be the leading producer in the technical product line serving a broad class of customer needs, imply product development, related innovations, and even unexpected additions that creativity may produce. In the multibusiness corporation, such as General Electric, broad goals, like being first or second in every industry in which it participates, leave the full development of a more specific business strategy to achieve or maintain that position in the hands of GE's division management. Determination of even more detailed goals falls to the managers of strategic business units. The definition of special character, a common set of values, and expectations for performance does not keep IBM, Hewlett-Packard, Xerox, and these days even General Motors, from being innovative.

Strategic planning is a legitimate staff activity, but strategic decision is a line function. Much information gathering, competitive intelligence, and exploration of required investment, costs, and potential return can come from good staff work. The decision process is properly presided over by the executives responsible, whose judgment is informed by, but is not confined to, quantitative analysis. Correction to analytical distortion comes from constant reference to corporate capability and to the relevance of proposed strate-

---

[2]See, for example, James Brian Quinn, "Strategic Goals: Process and Politics," *Sloan Management Review* (Fall 1977), pp. 21–37.

gic alternatives to company character and culture, either as they are or as, under leadership, they might become.

Our practitioner's theory, which you are asked to test, amend, or extend in the examination of the company situations you care about, postulates conceptually that strategy formulation and implementation should be allowed to interact. The formulation of strategy is not finished when implementation begins. Feedback from operations gives notice of changing environmental factors to which strategy should be adjusted. Unless it is to decline in competitiveness and performance, a business organization will change in response to the contribution of its new members, the changes in the markets and customer needs it services, and to success or failure in shaping its environment.

Implementation in the Innovative Corporation

The reciprocal relationship of strategy formulation and implementation makes middle management and employee involvement essential in both. To achieve planned results, goals must be known; to achieve superior results, these goals must be so wholly accepted that extraordinary effort or ingenuity, unforeseeable by distant planners, is induced. Sales or service persons often encounter in the field early clues to the need for change. In a company in which they doubt the interest of top management in responding, they may shrug their shoulders and shift their attention to other products. In a company oriented to innovation, they may report the opportunity through channels deliberately opened by people prepared to listen. The development of greater individual capability and the distinctive competence of a company that is the source of competitive advantage comes from experience, the successful solving of problems, and superior service to customers.

Such a moving capability will not occur unless companies acknowledge in their behavior, if not in so many words, that their purpose is as much to maintain and develop a cooperative and creative organization and to foster effective execution, as it is to lay plans and measure performance against plan. Committed team players can be involved in strategic determination by inviting their comment on the feasibility of strategic alternatives, when secrecy and security are not at stake. Resistance to change, which in such discussions often produces negative response to new ideas, can be used constructively by considering such objections before it is too late. Attempting to achieve amendment, acceptance, and understanding beforehand is more constructive than awaiting opposition later.

It becomes apparent that company organization structure and administrative policies and practices should permit and sustain involvement and a resultant commitment to company purposes. Being given a clearly defined job with lateral and upper limits becomes less and less attractive to present generations of educated employees and middle managers.[3] The values they bring to a company include independence, aversion to arbitrary or unreasoned authority, and ambition to do something important enough to deserve recognition. They expect to be treated as persons capable of responsibility and judgment. They will wish to have room to experiment and explore as they carry out their assignments and reach beyond them. If a company is to profit from their spontaneous contributions, it must involve them in the strategic planning process. One of the ways to do this is to go beyond exposing new possibilities for comment by asking such middle managers for a strategy for their division, department, section, or office and to deal sympathetically with the virtues and shortcomings of the outcome.

Your own experience offers many opportunities for such involvement. You can learn to observe the customary ways in which constructive engagement in strategic management is frustrated by what you may well conclude are archaic notions of authority, responsibility, hierarchy, status, and centralized decision making. Consider as you read this how much or how little the strategy of the company you know most about informs the thinking of the profit center, plant managers, and other midlevel managers—or their seniors, for that matter.

The structure of the innovative organization in which we expect people to make creative contributions must clearly be dominated by relevant aspects of the corporate strategy. The way in which the structure is administered will reflect the kind of organization deemed appropriate for the nature of the contribution expected. It is becoming clear that the corporation of the 21st century will be a different kind of organization from the giant, formally controlled, and relatively centralized company of the present. But before we examine that possibility, and before you use it in appraising and making recommendations for better performance in your own situation, we should consider what, by way of structure and process, needs to be done in a conventional late 1980s organization.

A reasonable profile of implementation activities goes as follows:

---

[3] D. Quinn Mills, in *The New Competitors* (New York: John Wiley and Sons, 1985), describes the expectations of what he calls the new generation of managers and the conflict between these and the traditional organization.

1. Once strategy is tentatively or finally set, the key tasks to be performed and kinds of decisions required must be identified.

2. Once the size of operations exceeds the capacity of one person, responsibility for accomplishing key tasks and making decisions must be assigned to individuals or groups. The division of labor must permit efficient performance of subtasks and must be accomplished by some hierarchical allocation of authority to assure achievement.

3. Formal provisions for the coordination of activities thus separated must be made in various ways, e.g., through a hierarchy of supervision, project and committee organizations, task forces, and other ad hoc units. The prescribed activities of these formally constituted bodies are not intended to preclude spontaneous voluntary coordination.

4. Information systems adequate for coordinating divided functions (i.e., for letting those performing part of the task know what they must know of the rest, and for letting those in supervisory positions know what is happening so that next steps may be taken) must be designed and installed.

5. The tasks to be performed should be arranged in a sequence comprising a program of action or a schedule of targets to be achieved at specified times. While long-range plans may be couched in relatively general terms, operating plans will often take the form of detailed budgets. These can meet the need for the establishment of standards against which short-term performance can be judged.

6. Actual performance, as quantitatively reported in information systems and qualitatively estimated through observation by supervisors and judgment of customers, should be compared to budgeted performance and to standards in order to test achievement, budgeting processes, the adequacy of the standards, and the competence of individuals.

7. Individuals and groups of individuals must be recruited and assigned to essential tasks in accordance with the specialized or supervisory skills they possess or can develop. At the same time, the assignment of tasks may be adjusted to the nature of available skills.

8. Individual performance, evaluated both quantitatively and qualitatively, should be subjected to influences (constituting a pattern of incentives) that will help to make it effective in accomplishing organizational goals.

9. Since individual motives are complex and multiple, incentives for achievement should range from those that are universally appealing—such as adequate compensation and an organizational climate favorable to the simultaneous satisfaction of individual and organizational purposes—to specialized forms of recognition, financial or nonfinancial, designed to fit individual needs and unusual accomplishments.

10. In addition to financial and nonfinancial incentives and rewards to motivate individuals to voluntary achievement, a system of constraints, controls, and penalties must be devised to contain nonfunctional activity and to enforce standards. Controls, like incentives, are both formal and informal. Effective control requires both quantitative and nonquantitative information, which must always be used together.

11. Provision for the continuing development of requisite technical and managerial skills is a high-priority requirement. The development of individuals must take place chiefly within the milieu of their assigned responsibilities. This on-the-job development should be supplemented by intermittent formal instruction and study.

12. Energetic personal leadership is necessary for continued growth and improved achievement in any organization. Leadership may be expressed in many styles, but it must be expressed in some perceptible style. This style must be natural and also consistent with the requirements imposed upon the organization by its strategy and membership.

Structure, Coordination, and Information Systems

The most fundamental processes that shape any organization structure consist of dividing the work and responsibility, coordinating the divided effort, and providing the essential information to enable people to do their part of the total job in ways that fit the whole. You will have studied elsewhere organization design and the management of information systems; we will not take up those subjects here. The implementation of corporate strategy requires that the division of responsibility facilitate the efficient performance of the key tasks identified by the strategy. The formal pattern by which tasks are identified and authority delegated should have visible relationship to corporate purpose, should fix responsibility in such a way as not to preclude teamwork, and should provide for the solution of problems as close to the point of action as possible.

In an organization governed by purpose, responsibility will usually exceed authority; the resulting ambiguity provides opportunity for initiative and clarification in terms of shared objectives rather than separate fiefdoms.

The specialization of function made necessary by the growth of an organization opens the door to counterstrategic departmental loyalties. Accountants behave like accountants and engineers like engineers more than is necessary. This specialized zeal has its advantages in the performance of a specialty, but can be frustrating to general managers when departmental biases and narrowness produce conflict or impede consensus in the consideration of critical issues. Functional specialists tend to interpret corporate purpose to suit themselves.

It follows, therefore, that in all organizations provision must be made to resolve differences in perspective, clarify strategy against misconceptions and special interpretations, and, above all, provide for discussion of alternatives that satisfy both departmental and organization needs. Committees, task forces, operations reviews, and planning meetings are the ordinary vehicles of common understanding. When such suborganizations are ill run, they are decried as time-wasting and unproductive and make strong-willed individuals impatient. In the hands of a skilled chairman, task forces and special purpose committees can be a principal source of creativity. The more informal the distribution of authority and the more ambiguous the boundaries between functions, the more important coordinating committees can become. The innovative company of the future provides much opportunity for people to talk to each other about what new undertakings should be launched, how they should be managed, and how old undertakings can be made more successful. Such meetings become more informative than the routine information provided to the organization by its reporting system.

The design of the formal structure of an organization will reflect corporate purpose, but it is the working of the informal organization that is not only central to productive cooperation but also will suggest what the formal structure should be. Landscape architects laying out sidewalks in a park or campus will wait to let people walk on the grass and then either pave the resulting paths or plant out superfluous or unacceptable routes. The entrepreneurial corporation begins in a small group of people whose understanding of what they are doing is constantly developed by close communication. What they are trying to accomplish is commanding; they have the resources to do only what most needs to be done. As such an organization grows, informality continues to dominate hierarchical distinctions, but eventually unclear separation of responsibility confuses people. The challenge becomes to clarify separate responsibilities without absolving the marketing people, for example, from knowing the strategically critical problems of production or product development.

The organization growing out of successful entrepreneurial chaos into a more structured company must somehow avoid the bureaucratic stultification that comes from mismanaged size and complexity.[4] Incentive and reward systems have to be developed to introduce fairness into what was intuitive recognition of the work of individual contributors once justified by daily observation no longer possible. But rigidity need not come on stage with systems. If the latter fall into the hands of bureaucrats who are technically educated in the intricacies of the system and dedicated to its extension for its own sake, then the relation of incentives, for example, to the kind of behavior that is most relevant to successful accomplishment of purpose is lost.

What an organization is trying to accomplish can be recognized if the formalities of hierarchical organization are kept to a minimum. Assignments should never be so clear or restrictive that persons cannot contribute, within the limits of their capability, what most needs to be done. Every functional assignment should include its relevance to corporate purpose; general management perspective can be assigned to persons by evaluating their performance in teamwork terms. Inquiries into new possibilities by interdepartmental task forces, in addition to their regular duties, should be a way of life for middle managers and professional people, just as quality circles are a symbol of innovative potential on the factory floor. Independent business units, skunk works, pilot operations, high-risk experiments in which failure without penalty is possible, competitive product championing, improvisatory off-budget product development—all characterize the innovative company.

It is my assumption that you would prefer a management career in an innovative company. In any case, the large American corporation in industries undergoing massive restructuring is remaking itself. The pressure for becoming slimmer, faster, more responsive, and more profitable may come more from the need for

---

[4] See James Brian Quinn, "Managing Innovation: Controlled Chaos," *Harvard Business Review* (May-June 1985), pp. 73 ff.

cost reduction under intense foreign competition and threat of takeover than from voluntary aspirations to excellence. But achieving or maintaining a position as a world-class company in selected market segments is an opportunity for any entrepreneur capable of devising an innovative strategy and developing an organization to extend the strategy and forestall the frustrations of formality, political conflict, and other aberrations of conventional organizations.

Commitment

The essence of successful implementation is commitment. Commitment comes from wanting to do something and from the satisfaction of having its importance recognized. As tasks become more difficult, wanting to contribute is not enough; greater capability is required. But most observers of established companies see a greater potential for cost reduction, product innovation, and quality enhancement than is ever fully recognized.[5] The effort to reexamine corporate capability can result in new ideas for at least minor additions to the product line or range of services, to quality, and to cost-effectiveness that cumulatively support or extend market share and help bond customers to their suppliers as partners.

Strategic management is thus now being redirected toward using and extending organizations' strengths and the innovative resilience of committed persons continually challenged to excel competitors and to improve on past performance. It becomes part of every manager's job. How well an organization can implement purpose becomes critical. Success depends on how much the persons assigned to achieve have been involved in the setting of goals and how deeply they have become committed to overcoming unexpected obstacles to success. They should not be deflected from common purpose by a company's organization structure or by its measurement, compensation, incentive and control systems.

But such systems are required. Informality cannot be absolute. Cooperation in a clearly understood common endeavor rarely occurs by chance. In the next chapter, we will look more closely at the processes through which commitment is expected to produce results. Look to your own experience to test, challenge, or reshape for your own use the ideas expressed here. You are in the process of deciding how you will make use of the concept of strategy and its

---

[5]For a research-based account of innovative practices in the management of work, see Richard E. Walton, "From Control to Commitment in the Workplace," *Harvard Business Review* (March-April 1985), pp. 77 ff.

power in shaping administrative systems toward relevance and simplicity in particular companies and unique situations. Nothing will help you more than examination of the real-life combinations of theory and reality in which you are caught up.

If you are not to attack your management responsibilities with a set of unrealistic textbook assumptions about how your associates should respond to your leadership or cooperation, you will think carefully about the need in any organization for clarity of mission, commitment to purpose, and careful preparation for changes in direction. Your awareness that strategy formulation and implementation must be interdependent simultaneous processes is fundamental to mastery of the art of management and indispensable to understanding the nature of organization.

Strategy as the Key to Simplicity

Strategy is conceived and implemented only in combinations of people to some degree "organized" or deployed in compatible task assignments. The strategy for each organization—in our conception of strategic management—will be in some ways unique, because of distinctiveness of competence and pervasion of values. The uniqueness of a company's strategy, in turn, is the key element in organization design. It is strategy, we have said, that should determine structure and the nature of the processes going on throughout the structure. This essential element of our conception puts an early end to our generalizations about how to organize. Until we know the strategy we cannot begin to specify the appropriate structure. This exposition cannot advise you whether a functional or divisional organization is appropriate to the strategy you will be working as a manager to implement, although it is clear that in growing and diversifying organizations the functional form will ordinarily precede the divisional and follow along as divisions are functionalized. Matrix management you can take or leave alone until you get to the situation itself; all you need to know now is that the key competing considerations—geographical specialization versus worldwide product management, for example—must somehow be integrated in a working equilibrium with strategic importance specifying the weights in the balance.

The elements of thinking like a general manager that we have recommended to you are inert until they are applied to the managerial circumstances in which you find yourself. The assignment of primacy to the application of an idea rather than to its elegant theoretical development is anathema to orthodox theorists. It is inconvenient for those persons expecting to be equipped with the latest and best tools for the solution of management problems and a jargon with which to demonstrate their sophistication. *But that the concept of strategy comes to full development only in the unique combination of circumstances in which any organization exists is a simplifying property of the idea that provides it much of its power in action.*

If you acquire the ability to think strategically, you will be able to lay aside the burdens of management conceived of as a science, which your education has laid upon you and tried to require you to remember. The more highly developed theories and propositions of most management sciences are either largely inapplicable or inappropriately applied, for they are usually presented by dedicated partisans as universally applicable. As a phenomenon of management the uniqueness of situations properly takes primacy over the substance of the management disciplines. As we are unable to tell you in detail how to design an organization until we know the purposes you are organizing for and the resources available, we can say there is no one best way to organize. At the same time the quest for purpose prevents organization aimlessness or drifting.

A related paradox presents itself as we consider the unlikelihood that the strategy we have said should always govern will be clear and complete at any one time. Because purpose evolves ordinarily over time as the components of strategy (environmental change and internal resources, for example) develop, it can dictate no final answer in terms of organization structure and process even in the situational context. The structure and processes in place will, in fact, affect the strategy. If you have profit centers, divisions, or subsidiaries charged with medium- and long-term success, they are likely to develop strategically significant innovations simply because divisionalization produces commitment to division rather than to parent organization. If you send fur buyers to Alaska instructed under quotas only to buy skins, they may end up selling groceries and other necessities to the trappers and incrementally make your fur business into a worldwide trading company. Strategy follows structure in real life, just as it sometimes precedes it there.

What is important now is that, in part, structure is strategy. If, in short, the process of strategy formulation is distributed throughout an organization, as it must be, the shape of that organization and the influences that motivate it will be reflected in the strategy it produces. The strategic decision must, of course, be made in the light of organization and human consequences. Furthermore, it must be arrived at recognizing the constraint of structure and systems derived from previous strategy that influence the generation of new alternatives. Context is both supportive and inhibiting. It may be necessary to change organization before certain strategic alternatives can be fully explored or experimentally attempted.

The subunits of an organization established to implement a given corporate purpose soon will develop divergent strategies to support their own growth and development, especially if responsibility for profit and growth has been assigned to those units. It is true, therefore, that the organization processes and measurement systems by which the functioning of the structure is evaluated will influence strategy. When an international company once tried to interest its Latin-American subsidiaries in profit rather than in the number of sewing machines sold, the country managers, inexperienced but responsive, began making ice cream, selling insurance, and manufacturing stove grates in unused plant space. These diversifications, all aimed at increasing profitability within one year, changed, at least for a time, the local strategy of this company. The structure—geographically discrete and relatively autonomous profit centers—and the incentive system—reward for short-run profitability—together could ultimately have changed the strategy of the entire company. As it happens, it was the corporate intention that the company go through a transition emphasizing profitability while its future strategy, too difficult a question for anybody in a company unused to strategic planning to settle, became a problem that could be managed.

Worldwide, the result of similar experiments was a company that faltered between being an appliance and electronics firm or an industrial and consumer products company without the resources or the organization form to make so wide a diversification work. The neglect of the sewing machine business, suffering under Japanese competition, and years of resulting losses led at long last to the dismissal of the responsible executive. He had known his company needed to be profit conscious, but he could not institutionalize a way to deal continuously with the decision of what businesses to be in.

The effective stimuli devised by this failed strategist sent the strategic process into a gallop in all directions. Strategy was made chaotic by change in organization structure and compensation systems. The country managers were neither provided with nor required to develop a new strategy for their areas. The outlines of a communicable corporate strategy were not generated at company headquarters to give coherent guidance to local initiatives.

Strategic management in the real world contends with the alternatives generated by organization form and the administrative processes affecting the motivation of people. While the uncertainties of decision about new alternatives delay clear-cut major changes in direction, hundreds of minor decisions incrementally may change the nature of the business and affect the character of the organization.

The real-life development of strategy must be superimposed upon the natural tendency of persons to "satisfice" (if you have read Herbert Simon) or (if you have not) to settle on the first satisfactory, rather than the best, solution to a problem. It envelops and influences the direction of the incrementalism by which organizations devise ad hoc responses to new occurrences. It extends the bounds of rationality within which persons and groups react to challenge from the market and social environment. It disciplines the bargaining that can characterize coalitions in organizations politicized by strategic uncertainty or dissatisfaction with the objectives and supporting policies in place.

The conclusion that attention to the conscious and deliberate choice of purpose can affect all aspects of an organization is in a sense a reassertion of the role in complex organizations of purposeful rationality. Strategy will evolve over time, no matter what. It will be affected by the consequences of its implementation. But the elucidation of goals can transcend incrementalism to make it a series of forays and experiments evaluated continuously against stated goals to result in the deliberate amendment of strategy or in the curtailment of strategic erosion. All organizations must be focused in purpose to avoid outstripping their resources or squandering their distinctive advantage.

The literature of organization theory is by itself, as we have said, of very little use in managing a live organization. What managers gain in discovering this fact is not that there is an advantage to being ignorant but that a powerful unitary idea can be developed in detail in a business situation they and their associates can know better than anybody else. Selection from what is available to educated generalists and known by specialists concentrating in techniques applicable to classes of narrow problems becomes effective when the relation of specialized knowledge to key problems of organization is recognized as strategically relevant. Knowledge of the evolving situation is more important and practicable than mastering the whole corpus of management book-learning. A rational procedure for comprehending the strategic posture of an organization, for seeing the intuitive purpose in its incremental development, and for assessing the extent to which its structure is effective in the performance of key tasks is much easier come by.

It requires experience, judgment, and skill, rather than general knowledge as such, for strategic management is and will remain more an art than a science. Artistic accomplishment depends heavily on the education, sensitivity, competence, and point of view of the artist. Simplicity is the essence of good art; the conception of strategy brings simplicity to complex organizations.

Chapter 7

The Implementation of Strategy: From Commitment to Results

Our study of strategy has brought us to the prescription that the way work and responsibility are divided, the choice of means for directing specialized attention to interdepartmental issues, and the design of information systems should not be allowed to divert attention from strategic goals. Structure should follow strategy, but structure once sufficiently well established to influence behavior and decision will then tend to arrange that strategy also follows structure. The latter tendency can go too far. Making flexibility and informality values of high rank, turning frequently to temporary ad hoc teams and task forces, involving specialists and interdepartmental inquiries—all help prevent organization structure from dominating and routinizing behavior. The effort to avoid the rigidity that limits the innovative capacity of static organizations means, for example, that job descriptions should never be regarded as anything more than a snapshot of the current status of a job designed to grow in responsibility as its performer grows in capability. The presumption in a developing organization is that as jobs expand with personal growth, routine activities can be delegated to junior persons, with activities requiring judgment and decision performed by fewer people at the senior level. The route to lean organizations is through expansion of responsibility, with higher levels of compensation rewarding the efforts of fewer people.

But deliberately checking the counterstrategic influence of bureaucratization will not in itself ensure that people assigned to different tasks in different locations will spontaneously choose the best course toward even those goals to which in principle they are all committed. They will not automatically seek the new skills they need as what they must accomplish becomes more complex. The innovative corporation is bent on preserving creativity, initiative, and the individual autonomy that makes original contribution possible. But even such an organization, one more typical of the 1990s than the 1970s, needs a set of administrative systems that will attempt equitable evaluation of performance, effective stimulus and reward for achievement, reasonable discipline and enforcement of policy, and development of managers, technical specialists, and producers at all levels.

The first purpose of such systems is to focus individual energy on organizational goals in such a way that individual goals are not needlessly thwarted. Another function of such systems is to acquaint new members of the organization, before they are qualified to be autonomous contributors to innovation, with the ways things are done currently, the kind of organization they have joined, and the standards by which they will be judged. A less attractive but necessary purpose is to constrain behavior that is irrelevant or destructive. Commitment to purpose will prosper if it is rewarded but founder if it is taken for granted or ignored.

One of the officers of the NIKE corporation, an extraordinarily successful marketer of athletic and leisure footwear and apparel, once made an interesting statement about the need of all contemporary organizations to communicate to young new-generation potential managers their requirements:

> Unless new employees, for example, are capable of assimilating NIKE expectations of centered hard work, and caring, creative thought, NIKE will stagger under the weight of a jet-setting, self-centered, arrogant—and average—middle management, who aggrandize themselves on a past they were not a part of, instead of striving for future successes in which they can share.

The processes we will look at have been studied and developed by specialists of several kinds. We will not attempt to summarize the state of the separate arts involved in influencing organizational behavior. We are concerned first with the limited but important ways in which the specialized bodies of knowledge can be put to use in the implementation of a given strategy rather than in the homogenization of organized activity. We will be suspicious of formality, rigidity, and uniformity, but remain mindful that policy in the management of human resources is necessary for fairness and equitable opportunity for growth and advancement, for protection of individuals against eccentric or biased management behavior, and for defense of corporate strategy against willful opportunists pursuing their own purpose.

Establishment of Standards and Measurement of Performance

In any organization the overall corporate strategy must be translated into detailed plans that permit comparison of actual to predicted performance. Whether standards are being set at exactly the proper level is never demonstrable. Commitment to attainment comes from negotiation to strike the balance between unreasonable expectations and unchallenged potential. Establishment of a plan will usually include improvement in performance over previous levels, but problems in the marketplace may make plans unattainable. Evidence that plans may not be achieved by the time predicted should prompt inquiry into the problem rather than immediate conclusion that performance is defective.

The most urgent duty of any manager is to see that properly planned results are accomplished. The pressure of this duty may lead to exaggerated respect for specific measures and the short-run results they quantify and thus to ultimate misevaluation of performance. Ready recourse to alibis and refusal to admit the validity of changed circumstances as excuse are just as inappropriate as is too quick a tendency to pass judgment rather than to take stock of the problem and to find new ways to deal with it.

Fallacy of the Single Criterion

The problems of measurement cluster about the fallacy of the single criterion. When any single measure like return on investment, for example, is used to determine the compensation, promotion, or reassignment of a manager, the resultant behavior will often lead to unplanned and undesired outcomes. No single measure can encompass the total contribution of an individual either to immediate and longer-term results or to the efforts of others. The sensitivity of individuals to evaluation leads them to produce the performance that will measure up in terms of the criterion rather than in terms of more important purposes. Since managers respond to the measures management actually takes to reward performance, mere verbal exhortations to behave in the manner required by long-range strategy carry no weight and cannot be relied upon to preclude undesirable actions encouraged by a poorly designed measurement and reward system.

Faith in the efficacy of a standard measure like return on

investment can reach extreme proportions, especially among managers to whom the idea of strategy is apparently unfamiliar. Instances in which performance is measured in terms of just one figure or ratio are so numerous as to suggest that the pursuit of quantification and measurement as such has overshadowed the real goal of management evaluation. If we return to our original hypothesis that profit and return on investment are terms that can be usefully employed to denote the results to be sought by business, but are too general to characterize its distinctive mission or purpose, then we must say that *short-term profitability is not by itself an adequate measure of managerial performance.* Return on investment, when used alone, is a dangerous criterion because it can lead business people to postpone needed product research or the modernization of facilities in the interest of keeping down the investment on the basis of which their performance is measured. We must conclude that evaluation of performance must not be focused exclusively upon the criterion of short-run profitability or any other single standard that may cause managers to act contrary to the long-range interests of the company as a whole.

Need for Multiple Criteria

As you take a new look at the evaluation systems in which you are enmeshed, you will be concerned with developing better criteria. Our concern for strategy naturally leads us to suggest that the management evaluation system that plays so great a part in influencing management performance must employ a number of criteria, some of which are subjective and thus difficult to quantify. It is easy to argue that subjective judgments are unfair. But use of a harmful or irrelevant criterion just because it lends itself to quantification is a poor exchange for alleged objectivity.

If multiple criteria are to be used, it is not enough for top management simply to announce that short-term profitability and return on investment are only two measures among many—including responsibility to society—by which executives are going to be judged. To give subordinates freedom to exercise judgment and simultaneously to demand profitability produce an enormous pressure that cannot be effectively controlled by endless talk about tying rewards to factors other than profit.

The tragic predicament of people who, though upright in other ways, engage in bribery, "questionable payments," price fixing, and subtler forms of corruption and of their superiors who are often unaware of these practices should dramatize one serious flaw of the profit center form of organization. Characteristically, management expects this format to solve the problems of evaluation by decentralizing freedom of decision to subordinates so long as profit objectives are met. Decentralization seems sometimes to serve as a cloak for nonsupervision, except for the control implicit in the superficial measure of profitability. It would appear to preclude accurate evaluation, and the use of multiple criteria may make a full measure of decentralization inappropriate.

Effective Evaluation of Performance

To delegate authority to profit centers and to base evaluation upon profit performance must not mean that the profit center's strategic decisions are left unsupervised. *Even under decentralization, top management must remain familiar with divisional substrategy, with the fortunes—good and bad—that attend implementation, and with the problems involved in attempting to achieve budgeted performance.* The true function of measurement is to increase perceptions of the problems limiting achievement. If individuals see where they stand in meeting schedules, they may be led to inquire why they are not somewhere else. If this kind of question is not asked, the answer is not proffered. An effective system of evaluation must include information that will allow top management to understand the problems faced by subordinates in achieving the results for which they are held responsible. And if evaluation is to be comprehensive enough to avoid the distortions cited thus far, immediate results will not be the only object of evaluation. The effectiveness with which problems are handled along the way will be evaluated, even though this judgment, like most of the important decisions of management, must remain subjective.

The process of formulating and implementing strategy, which may be supervised directly by the chief executive in a single-unit company, can be shared widely in a multiunit company. It can be the theme of the information exchanged between organization levels. Preoccupation with final results need not be so exclusive as to prevent top management from working with divisional management in establishing objectives and policies or in formulating plans to meet objectives. Such joint endeavor helps to ensure that divisional performance will not be evaluated without full knowledge of the problems encountered in implementation.

When the diversified company becomes so large that this process is impracticable, new means must be devised. *Implicit in accurate evaluation is familiarity with performance on a basis other than accounting figures.*

A shared interest in the problems to be overcome in successfully implementing departmental and individual strategies makes possible a kind of communication, an accuracy of evaluation, and a constructive influence on behavior that cannot be approached by application of a single criterion. For one manager as for a whole company, the quality of objectives and of subsequent attempts to overcome obstacles posed by circumstance and by competition is the most important aspect of a manager's performance to be evaluated.

Motivation and Incentives

The influences upon behavior in any organization are visible and invisible, planned and unplanned, formal and informal. The intent to measure affects the performance that is the object of measurement; cause and effect obscure each other. The executive who refuses to leave the implementation of strategy to chance has available diverse means of encouraging behavior that advances strategy and deterring behavior that does not. The positive elements, always organized in patterns that make them influential in given situations, may be designated as motivation and incentive systems. The negative elements, similarly patterned, can be grouped as systems of restraint and control. Organization studies have led their authors variously to prefer positive or negative signals and to conclude that one or the other is preferable. The general manager will do well to conclude that each is indispensable.

Executive Compensation

Whatever the necessity for and the difficulties of performance evaluation, the effort to encourage and reward takes precedence over the effort to deter and restrain. Thus, properly directed, incentives may have more positive effects than control. Certainly, general manager-strategists, whose own experiences are likely to have made them interested in executive compensation, should welcome whatever guidance they can get from researchers or staff assistants working in the field of job evaluation and compensation. Unfortunately, here also the prevailing thinking is often oriented less toward the goals to be sought than toward the requirements of the systems adopted.

Executives, like workers, are influenced by nonmonetary as well as financial incentives. At the same time, financial rewards are very important, and much thought has been given to equitable compensation of executives.

Unfortunately for the analyst of executive performance, it is harder to describe for executives than for machine operators what they do and how they spend their time. The terminology of job descriptions is full of phrases like "has responsibility for," "maintains relationships with," and "supervises the operation of." The activities of planning, problem solving, and directing or administering are virtually invisible. And recruiting, training, and developing subordinates are hardly more concretely identifiable.

In any case, it is fallacious to assume that quality of performance is the only basis for the compensation of executives. Many other factors must be taken into account. The job itself has certain characteristics that help to determine pay schedules. These include complexity of the work, general education required, and knowledge or technical training needed. Compensation also reflects the responsibility of job-incumbents for people and property, the nature and number of decisions they must make, and the effect of their activities and decisions upon profits.

In addition to reflecting the quality of performance and the nature of the job, an executive's compensation must also have some logical relationship to rewards paid to others in the same organization. That is, the compensation system must reflect in some way a person's position in the status system. On any one ladder there must be suitable steps between levels from top to bottom, if incentive is to be provided and increased scope recognized. At the same time, adjustments must be made to reflect the varying contributions that can be expected from individuals in the status system of the staff versus the line.

Furthermore, in a compensation system, factors pertaining to the individual are almost as important as those pertaining to performance, the job, or the structure of the organization. People's age and length of service, the state of their health, some notion of their future potential, some idea of their material needs, and some insight into their views about all of these should influence either the amount of total pay or the distribution of total pay among base salary, bonuses, stock options, and other incentive measures.

Besides the many factors already listed, still another set of influences—this time from the environment—ordinarily affects the level of executive compensation. Included here are regional differences in the cost of living, increments allowed for overseas assignment, market price of given qualifications and experience, level of local taxation, desire for tax avoidance or delay, and effect of high business salaries on other professions.

Just as multiple criteria are appropriate for the evaluation of performance, so many considerations must be taken into account in the compensation of executives. The company that says it pays only for results does not know what it is doing.

Role of Incentive Pay

In addition to the problem of deciding which factors to reward, there is the equally complex issue of deciding which forms compensation should take. No matter how great the enthusiasm of people for their work, attention to the level of executive salary is an important ingredient in the achievement of strategy. Even after the desired standard of living is attained, money is still an effective incentive. Businesspeople used to the struggle for profit find satisfaction in their own growing net worth.

There is no question about the desirability of paying high salaries for work of great value. In addition, profit sharing, executive bonuses, stock options, performance shares, stock purchase plans, deferred compensation contracts, pensions, insurance, savings plans, and other fringe benefits have multiplied enormously. Regarded as incentives to reward individual performance, many of these devices encounter two immediate objections. First, how compatible are the assumptions behind such rewards with the aspirations of the business person to be viewed as a professional? What kind of executive will perform better with a profit-sharing bonus than with an equivalent salary? We may ask whether doctors should be paid according to longevity of their patients and whether surgeons would try harder if given a bonus when their patients survived an operation. Second, how feasible is it to distinguish any one individual's contribution to the total accomplishment of the company? Even if the contribution could be distinguished and correctly measured, what are the implications of the fact that the funds available for added incentive payments came from total rather than individual performance? In view of these considerations, it can at least be argued that incentives for individual performance reflect doubtful assumptions.

If, then, incentives are ruled out as an inappropriate or impractical means of rewarding individual effort, should they be cast out altogether? I believe not. There is certainly merit in giving stock options or performance shares to the group of executives most responsible for strategy decisions, if the purpose is to assure reward for attention to the middle and longer run future. There is some rationale for giving the same group current or even deferred bonuses, the amount of which is tied to annual profit, if the purpose is to motivate better cost control. Certainly, too, incentive payments to the key executive group must be condoned where needed to attract and hold the scarce managerial talent without which any strategy will suffer.

In any case, as you examine the effort made by your own company to provide adequate rewards, to stimulate effective executive performance, and to inspire commitment to organizational purposes, you will wish to look closely at the relation between the incentive offered and the kind of performance needed. This observation holds as true for nonmonetary as it does for financial rewards.

Nonmonetary Incentives

The area of nonmonetary incentive systems is even more difficult to traverse quickly than that of financial incentives. Executives, as human as other employees, are as much affected as anyone else by pride in accomplishment, climate for free expression, pleasure in able and honest associates, and satisfaction in work worth doing.

The climate most commonly extolled by managers is one in which they have freedom to experiment and apply their own ideas without unnecessary constraints. Given clear objectives and a broad consensus, latitude can be safely granted to executives to choose their own course—so long as they do not conceal the problems they encounter. In other words, executives can be presumed to respond to the conditions likely to encourage the goal-oriented behavior expected of them.

We may not always know the influence exerted by evaluation, compensation, and promotion, but if we keep purpose clear and incentive systems simple, we may keep unintended distractions to a minimum. Above all, we should be able to see the relevance to desired outcomes of the rewards offered. The harder it is to relate achievement to motives, the more cautious we should be in proposing an incentives program.

Constraints and Control

Like the system of incentives, the system of restraints and controls should be designed with the requirements of strategy in mind, rather than the niceties of complex techniques and procedures. It is the function of penalties and controls to enforce rather than to encourage—to inhibit strategically undesirable behavior rather than to create new patterns. Motivation is a complex of both positive and negative influences. Working in conjunction, these induce desired performance and inhibit undesirable behavior.

The need for controls—even at the executive level—is rooted in the central facts of organization itself. The inevitable consequence of divided activity is the emergence of substrategies, which are at least slightly deflected from the true course by the needs of individuals and the concepts and procedures of specialized groups, each with its own quasi-professional precepts and ideals. We must have controls, therefore, even in healthy and competent organizations manned by people of goodwill who are aware of organization purpose.

Formal Control

Like other aspects of organizational structure and processes, controls may be both formal and informal, both prescribed and emergent. Both types are needed, and both are important. It is, however, in the nature of things that management is more likely to give explicit attention to the formal controls that it has itself prescribed than to the informal controls emergent within particular groups or subgroups.

Formal and informal controls differ in nature as well as in their genesis. The former have to do with quantifiable data, the latter with subjective values and behavior. Formal control derives from accounting; it reflects the conventions and assumptions of that discipline and implies the prior importance of what can be quantified over what cannot. Its influence arises from the responsiveness of individuals—if subject to supervision and appraisal—to information that reveals variances between what is recorded as being expected of them and what is recorded as being achieved. If the information depicts variances from strategically desirable behavior, then it tends to direct attention toward strategic goals and to support goal-oriented policy. But if, as is more often the case, the information simply focuses on those short-run results the state of the art can measure, then it directs effort toward performance that, if not undesirable, is at least biased toward short-run objectives.

To emphasize the probable shortcomings of formal or quantifiable controls is not to assert they have no value. Numbers do influence behavior—especially when pressures are applied to subordinates by superiors contemplating the same numbers. Numbers are essential in complex organizations because personal acquaintance with what is being accomplished and personal surveillance over it by an owner-manager is no longer possible. As we have seen, the performance of individuals and subunits cannot be left to chance, even when acceptance and understanding of policy have been indicated and adequate competence and judgment are assured. Whether for surveillance from above or for self-control and self-guidance, numbers have a meaningful role to play, and well-selected numbers have a very meaningful role. We in no way mean to diminish the importance of figures, but only to emphasize that numerical measurement must be supplemented by informal or social controls.

Integrating Formal and Social Control

Just as the idea of formal control is derived from accounting, the idea of informal control is derived from the inquiries of the behavioral sciences into the nature of organizational behavior. In all functioning groups, norms develop to which individuals are responsive if not obedient. These norms constitute the accepted way of doing things; they define the limits of proper behavior and the type of action that will meet with approval from the group. In view of the way they operate, the control we have in mind is better described as *social* or *cultural* rather than *informal.* It is embedded in the activities, interactions, and sentiments characterizing group behavior. Sentiments take the form of likes and dislikes among people and evaluative judgments exercised upon each other. Negative sentiments, of great importance to their objects, may be activated by individual departure from a norm; such sentiments can either constitute a punishment in themselves or can lead to some other form of punishment.

The shortcomings of formal control based on quantitative measurements of performance can be largely obviated by designing and implementing a system in which formal and social controls are integrated. For example, meetings of groups of managers to discuss control reports can facilitate inquiry into the significance of problems lying behind variances, can widen the range of solutions considered, and can bring pressure to bear from peers as well as from superiors. All these features can in turn contribute to finding a new course of action that addresses the problem rather than the figures.

Enforcing Ethical Standards

One of the most vexing problems in attempting to establish a functional system of formal and social controls lies in the area of ethical standards. In difficult competitive situations, the pressure for results can lead individuals into illegal and unethical practices. Instead of countering this tendency, group norms may encourage yielding to these pressures. For example, knowing that others were doing the same thing undoubtedly influenced highly competitive branch managers, rewarded for profit, in the national brokerage firm referred to earlier, to overdraft systematically their bank accounts to secure, in effect, interest-free loans to invest. Recurring violations of price-fixing regulations, in industries beset by over-capacity and aggressive competition, are sometimes responses to pressures to meet sales and profit expectations of a distant home office.

When top management refuses to condone pursuit of company goals by unethical methods, it must resort to penalties like dismissal that are severe enough to dramatize its opposition. If a division sales manager who is caught having arranged prostitution for an important customer against both the standards of expected behavior and the policy of the company is not penalized at all, or only mildly, because of the volume of his sales and the profit he generates, ethical standards will not long be of great importance. If he is fired, then his successor is likely to think twice about the choice of means to achieve the organizational purposes assigned. When, as has happened, a regional vice president of a large insurance firm is fired for misappropriating $250,000 of expense money, but is retained as a consultant because he controls several millions of revenue, mixed signals confuse the communication but call attention to the dilemmas of enforcement.

But there are limits to the effectiveness of punishment, in companies as well as in families and in society. If violations are not detected, the fear of punishment tends to weaken. A system of inspection is therefore implicit in formal control. But besides its expense and complexity, such policing of behavior adversely affects the attitudes of people toward their organizations. Their commitment to creative accomplishment is likely to be shaken, especially if they are the kind of persons who are not likely to cut corners in the performance of their duties. To undermine the motivation of the ethically inclined is a high price to pay for detection of the weak. It is the special task of the Internal Audit function and the Audit Committee of the corporate board of directors not only to make investigation more effective but also to minimize its negative police-state connotations and distortions.

The student of general management is thus confronted by a dilemma: if an organization is sufficiently decentralized to permit individuals to develop new solutions to problems and new avenues to corporate achievement, then the opportunity for wrongdoing cannot be eliminated. This being so, a system of controls must be supplemented by a selective system of executive recruitment and training. No system of control, no program of rewards and penalties, no procedures of measuring and evaluating performance can take the place of the individual who has a clear idea of right and wrong, a consistent personal policy, and the strength to stand the gaff when results suffer because he or she stands firm. His or her development is greatly assisted by the systems that permit the application of qualitative criteria and avoid the oversimplification of numerical measures. It is always the way systems are administered that determines their ultimate usefulness and impact.

Recruitment and Development of Management

Organizational behavior consistent with the accomplishment of purpose is the product of interacting *systems* of measures, motives, standards, incentives, rewards, penalties, and controls. Put another way, behavior is the outcome of *processes* of measurement, evaluation, motivation, and control. These systems and processes affect and shape the development of all individuals, most crucially those in management positions. Management development is therefore an ongoing process in all organizations, whether planned or not. It is appropriate, however, to inquire into the need to plan this development, rather than to let it occur as it will.

The supply of men and women who, of their own volition, can or will arrange for their own development is smaller than required. Advances in technology, the internationalization of markets, the progress of research on information processing, and, above all, the unexplored territory into which the innovative corporation will repeatedly venture make it absurd to suppose that persons can learn all they will need to know from what they are currently doing. In particular, the activities of the general manager differ so much in kind from those of other management that special preparation for the top job should be considered. In addition to assignment to a planned succession of jobs in different areas, this may include attendance at university programs of executive education, custom-tailored opportunity to study business-government relationships, or membership on the board of another company or public service organization.

Strategy can be our guide to (1) the skills that will be required to perform the critical tasks; (2) the number of persons with specific skill, age, and experience characteristics who will be required in the light of planned growth and predicted attrition; and (3) the number of new individuals of requisite potential who must be recruited to ensure the availability, at the appropriate time, of skills that require years to develop.

No matter what the outcome of these calculations, it can safely be said that every organization must actively recruit new talent if it aims to maintain its position and to grow. These recruits should have adequate ability not only for filling the junior positions to which they are initially called, but also for learning the management skills needed to advance to higher positions. Like planning of all kinds, recruiting must be done well ahead of actual need. The choice of new members of an organization may be the most crucial function of management development and the most telling test of judgment.

The labor force requirements imposed by commitment to a strategy of growth mean quite simply that men and women over-qualified for conventional beginning assignments must be sought and carefully cultivated. Individuals who respond well to the opportunities devised for them should be assigned to established organization positions and given responsibility as fast as capacity to absorb it is indicated. To promote rapidly is not the point so much as to maintain the initial momentum and to provide work to highly qualified individuals that is both essential and challenging. The innovative company will find challenge for rapidly developing competence; it cannot remain innovative without doing so.

Continuing Education

The rise of professional business education and the development of advanced management programs make formal training available to men and women not only at the beginning of their careers but also at appropriate intervals thereafter. Short courses for executives are almost always stimulating and often of permanent value. But management development as such is predominantly an organizational process that must be supported, not thwarted, by the incentive and control systems to which we have already alluded. Distribution of rewards and penalties will effectively determine how much attention executives will give to the training of their subordinates. No amount of lip service will take the place of action in establishing effective management development as an important management activity. To evaluate managers in part on their effort and effectiveness in bringing along their juniors requires subjective measures and a time span longer than one fiscal year. These limitations do not seriously impede judgment, especially when both strategy and the urgency of its implications for manpower development are clearly known.

In designing on-the-job training, a focus on strategy makes possible a substantial economy of effort, in that management development and management evaluation can be carried on together.

The evaluation of performance can be simultaneously administered as an instrument of development. For example, any manager could use a conference with his superiors not only to discuss variances from budgeted departmental performance, but also to discover how far his or her suggested solutions are appropriate or inappropriate and why. In all such cases, discussion of objectives proposed, problems encountered, and results obtained provide opportunities for inquiry, for instruction and counsel, for learning what needs to be done and at what level of effectiveness.

Besides providing an ideal opportunity for learning, concentration on objectives permits delegation to juniors of choice of means and other decision-making responsibilities otherwise hard to come by. Throughout the top levels of the corporation, if senior management is spending adequate time on the surveillance of the environment and on the study of strategic alternatives, then the responsibility for day-to-day operations must necessarily be delegated. Since juniors cannot learn how to bear responsibility without having it, this necessity is of itself conducive to learning. If, within limits, responsibility for the choice of means to attain objectives is also delegated, opportunity is presented for innovation, experimentation, and creative approaches to problem solving. Where ends rather than means are the object of attention and agreement exists on what ends are and should be, means may be allowed to vary at the discretion of the developing junior manager. The clearer the company's goals, the smaller the emphasis that must be placed on uniformity, and the greater the opportunity for initiative. Freedom to make mistakes and achieve success is more productive in developing executive skills than practice in following detailed how-to-do-it instructions designed by superiors or staff specialists. Commitment to purpose rather than to procedures appears to energize initiative.

Management Development and Corporate Purpose

A stress on purpose rather than on procedures suggests that organizational climate, though intangible, is more important to individual growth than the mechanisms of human resource management. The development of each individual in the direction best suited both to his or her own powers and to organizational needs is most likely to occur in the company where everybody is encouraged to work at the height of his or her ability and is rewarded for doing so. Such a company must have a clear idea of what it is and what it intends to become. With this idea sufficiently institutionalized so that organization members grow committed to it, the effort re quired for achievement will be forthcoming without elaborate incentives and coercive controls. Purpose, especially if considered worth accomplishing, is the most powerful incentive to accomplishment. If goals are not set high enough, they must be reset—as high as developing creativity and accelerating momentum suggest.

In short, from the point of view of general management, management development is not a combination of staff activities and formal training designed to provide neophytes with a common body of knowledge or to produce a generalized good manager. Rather, development is inextricably linked to organizational purpose, which shapes to its own requirements the kind, rate, and amount of development that takes place. It is a process by which men and women are professionally equipped to be—as far as possible in advance of the need—what the evolving strategy of the firm requires them to be, at the required level of excellence.

Chief executives will have their own special interest in the process of management development. Standards of performance, measures for accurate evaluation, incentives, and controls will have a lower priority in their eyes than a committed organization, manned by people who know what they are supposed to do and are committed to the overall ends to which their particular activities contribute.

Chapter 8

Strategic Management and Corporate Governance

We have now quite carefully explored the concepts and subconcepts essential to the conscious formulation and implementation of a strategy governing the planned development of a total organization. It becomes appropriate at this point to return to the view of corporate strategy as an organizational process forever in motion, never ending. The merger of the process and substantive content of the concept of strategy will take us to the principal problems of corporate governance and the expanding responsibility of the board of directors.

Strategy as a Process

For the purposes of analysis, it is reasonable to consider strategy formulation complete before implementation begins, as if it made sense to know where we are going before we start. Yet we know that we often move without knowing where we will end up; the determination of purpose is in reality in dynamic interrelation with its implementation. Implementation is itself a complex process including many subprocesses of thought and organization that introduce tentativeness and doubt into prior resolution and lead us to change direction.

That strategy formulation is itself a *process of organization,* rather than the masterly conception of a single mind, must finally become clear. I made this suggestion when we were considering organization design. Many facts of life conspire to complicate the simple notion that persons or organizations should decide what they can, want, and should do and then do it. The sheer difficulty of recognizing and reconciling uncertain environmental opportunity, unclear corporate capabilities and limited resources, submerged personal values, and emerging aspirations to social responsibility suggests that, at least in complicated organizations, strategy must be an organizational achievement and may often be unfinished. Important as leadership is, the range of strategic alternatives that must be considered in a decentralized or diversified company exceeds what one person can conceive of. As technology develops, chief executives cannot usually maintain their own technical knowledge at the level necessary for accurate personal critical discriminations. As a firm extends its activities internationally, the senior executive in the company cannot personally learn in detail the cultural and geographical conditions that require local adaptation of both ends and means.

As in all administrative processes, managing the process becomes a function distinct from performing it. The principal strategists of technically or otherwise complex organizations manage a strategic decision-making process rather than make strategic decisions. When they "make" a decision approving proposals originating from appraisals of need and opportunity made by others, they are ratifying decisions emerging from lower echelons in which the earliest and most junior participants may have played importantly decisive roles. The structure of the organization, as observed earlier, may predetermine the nature of subsequent changes in strategy. In this sense strategy formulation is an activity widely shared in the hierarchy of management, rather than being concentrated at its highest levels.

Participation in strategy formulation may begin with the market manager who sees a new product opportunity or the analyst who first arranges the assumptions that make possible a desirable return on investment in a new venture. Because of the response to reward and punishment systems considered earlier, the strategic alternatives generated in autonomous corporate units may be the product of competition for limited resources or of divisional empire building.

The strategy process, with its evolutionary, structural, analytical, and emotional components, encounters the real-life challenges for which conscious professional management has been devised. Opportunism remains the principal counter force; it need not be put down altogether, for it can be turned to good use. In the course of an established strategy, changing only imperceptibly in response to changing capabilities and market environments, sudden opportunity or major tactical decision may intrude to distract attention from distant goals and direct it to immediate gain. Thus, the opportunity for a computer firm to merge with a large finance company may seem too good to pass up, but the strategy of the company will change with the acquisition or its ability to implement its strategy will be affected. A strategy may suddenly be rationalized to mean something very different from what was originally intended because of the opportunism that, at the beginning of this book, we declared the conceptual enemy of strategy. The necessity to accommodate unexpected opportunity in the course of continuous strategic decision is a crucial aspect of process. Accepting or refusing specific opportunity will strengthen or weaken the capability of an organization and thus alter what is probably the most crucial determinant of strategy in an organization with already developed market power.

Managing the Process

It is clear then that the strategic process should not be left untended. The first step is acceptance of the need for a continuous process of strategic decision as the basis for management action. This process extends from the origin of a discrete decision to its successful completion and incorporation into subsequent decisions. With this need established in an organization, the next step is to initiate the process and secure the participation first of those in senior management positions and then of those in intermediate and junior positions. The simplest way for the chief executive of a company to begin is to put corporate objectives on the agenda of appropriate meetings of functional staff, management, or directors.

Consider, for example, a large, long-established, diversified, and increasingly unprofitable company in an old industry. Its principal division was fully integrated from ownership of sources of raw materials to delivery of manufactured products to the consumer. Its president, after a day's discussion of the concept of strategy, asked his seven vice presidents, who had worked together for years, to submit to him a one-page statement expressing each officer's concept of the company's business, a summary statement of its strategy. He had in mind to go on from there, as users of this book must do. After identifying the strategy deducible from the company's established operations and taking advantage of their participation in resource allocation decisions, the president would then ask the vice presidents to evaluate the apparent current strategy and make suggestions for its change and improvement. This first effort to establish a conscious process of strategic decision came to a quick recess when the president found that it took weeks to get the statements submitted and that, once collected, they read like descriptions of seven different companies.

When discussion of current strategy resumed, a number of key issues emerged from a study of a central question—why so successful a company was seeing its margins shrink and its profits decline. The communication of similar issues to those assigned responsibility to deal with the functions the issues affect was an obvious next step. The soundness of the company's recent diversification was assigned as a question to the division managers concerned. They were asked to present a strategy for a scheduled achievement of adequate return or of orderly divestment. The alternative uses of the company's enormous resources of raw material were examined for the first time. The record of the research and development department, venerable in the industry for former achievements, was suddenly seen to be of little consequence in the competition that had taken away market share. Decisions long since postponed or ignored began to seem urgent. Two divisions were discontinued and expectations of improved performance began to alter the attention of division and functional managers throughout the organization to strategic issues.

Recent corporate experience has refined the straightforward but amateurish approach just summarized. Recognition that corporate strategy in complex organizations is the outcome of organization process rather than unilateral decision has important specific consequences. Variations in perception mean that the strategy in place takes different forms for different persons in organization units. Discovery of these differences may ignite conflict; the attempt to resolve them may be threatening to people committed to old undertakings newly submitted to critical scrutiny. The politicized rivalry for resources must become openly related not to personal influence or to division or departmental interests, but to corporate purposes. The need for cross-divisional or multifunctional cooperation in the development of new products or services will alter the boundaries of entrenched definitions of responsibility. Asking people to question the present validity of past practices comes as a shock to organizations never so challenged before. Above all, the process needs leadership, direction, and visibility. Otherwise, incremental pursuits of individual and departmental self-interest will result in a sprawling attenuation of strength vulnerable to attack by better-focused competitors.

All the impediments to the reexamination of present strategy, the identification of strategic issues, the generation of new strategic alternatives, and the decision to change direction are understandable. But to be understood to the point of remedy, they must be identified. To be surmounted, they must be discussed under leadership seeking progress. The discussion must include perceptions of the character of the company and the emotional as well as the rational bases for preferring one definition of the company's core business to another.

The approach to engaging the key members of any organization in the reexamination of its strategy and the reaffirmation (or more likely the redirection) must vary from organization to organization. But the common elements of an approach currently being undertaken by firms of many different kinds can be roughly identified. The guide that follows is intended to be suggestive of aspects of a process that will be as unique to an individual company as its strategy should be.

1. *Recognition of a problem.* If performance has faltered and the reasons for the decline can be identified as a widening gap between a company's choice of products and markets and the changing preferences and needs of its customers or as a loss of competitive strength, then a problem exists that can be made a matter of general concern. If a chief executive officer is concerned about anything of major import, that unrest commands attention. It will hold attention if it is documented as serious. If the problem is personal performance rather than obsolescent strategy, then replacement of persons rather than change of direction may be necessary.

2. *Designation of responsibility for inquiry.* When discussion of the problem by the CEO and his or her associates suggests that a strategic review and redirection are necessary, a person is designated as director or coordinator of the inquiry. When the organization is so large that the CEO cannot undertake this assignment, then a member of his or her staff—a director of corporate development or strategic planning, or a senior vice president of suitable breadth of experience—is asked to lead the inquiry.

3. *Interviews with line and staff managers.* The designated head of the inquiry interviews all the senior line and staff executives of the company. Who is key depends on the scope of responsibility and size of company. If the number of persons to be interviewed is large, then usually consultants of appropriate experience are engaged to help. Such consultants should be

skilled in helping companies decide rather than in making recommendations based on industry knowledge or market research alone.

The information sought in these interviews begins with the manager's view of the company and his or her concept of its mission and its future. This view should include not only the economic mission but also the company as a place to work and as a career opportunity for its managerial and other employees. The manager's perception of the company's strategic problem and his or her ideas about its origin and solutions should be recorded without argument.

When the interviews with the chosen managers are completed, it is sometimes appropriate to present to the interviewees as a group the varied results of the interviews. The CEO may not be comfortable in presiding at such a meeting. (This in itself might be a symptom of a problem.) In that case the director of the inquiry should lead the discussion. The object should be to acquaint those present with the variety of concepts of mission and to clarify the most important common and divergent elements. The probable need to focus on those products and services in which the company excels should result in the realization that painful choices are required.

If all that is not thought enough as a beginning, how the inquiry should proceed should be discussed. The CEO may wish to indicate his or her own determination with respect to the outcome of subsequent discussion. The CEO's dismay, if any, should not be voiced except as indicating the urgency of further exploration of what should be done. His or her ideas of the outcome, while no doubt becoming more clear, should not be announced. They must remain tentative or the strategic process will be a sham and soon seen as such. Candor, openmindedness, and interest in new ideas should be encouraged by the leader of the discussion.

4. *Staff examination of strategic alternatives.* Either with internal staff or with supplemental consulting, the identification of the current strategy should be independently undertaken. It should be examined in the light of performance against competition and validity against market trends. Portfolio analysis to classify the company's businesses according to market share and projected growth of market is often appropriate. Company financial projections of current strategy should be critically examined. The direction of external research depends on the nature of the company's problem and the strategic issues that have been revealed.

The staff external inquiry should culminate in a choice of alternative definitions of its business, the size and kind of company it can or may wish to be. These alternatives will relate to what has been discovered by interview and to the varying estimates of the company's capability. No recommendations should be implicit in the presentation of alternatives. The objective is to prepare an agenda for decision in a climate made receptive by the way in which the inquiry has been conducted.

5. *Strategic review conference.* After the alternatives have been considered by the key staff and line managers, a session of several days is usually held to discuss the alternatives and their implications. It is almost inevitable that the discussion will produce attractive modifications of the alternatives or even new alternatives not previously explored. The extent to which the alternatives have been documented will determine how close to consensus it is appropriate to come. The appearance of objections to the alternatives will offer clues to implementation problems.

Members of the board of directors are often invited to such conferences. It must be clear that their participation is as individuals and they are present to be able to react to what is eventually submitted to them by the chief executive. It may be appropriate for the CEO to express his or her reaction to the discussion and to the alternatives, but decision should not be taken at this conference. How the decision will be reached, if known, should be stated.

6. *Approach to final decision.* The conference will probably reveal conflicts or uncertainties that need to be further explored. If, however, decision has become clear, the CEO is nearly ready to make recommendations to the board. If the outcome is still unclear, the CEO may want to set up a small group of managers, who have shown themselves productive participants in the process, as an advisory group but not a management committee. Under the chairmanship of the CEO, meetings would be held until decision can be reached about the initial resolution of strategic issues and continuation of the current attack on the perceived problem. Options will be kept open where uncertainty requires further experience or experiment. If a company is engaged in more than one business, then the division or department manager should be asked to submit

strategies for examination of fit and consistency by the strategy advisory group. Divisional plans would stem from approved strategy statements.

Report to the board of the progress of these discussions and their outcome would continue until final recommendations are made. The strategy group would continue to function as new initiatives are put in place and could well become the monitor of the process. That the CEO would chair or attend meetings of this group would ensure recurrent top management attention to the need for innovation and adaptation. Although its function would be to cope with the strategic implications of operating results, this group should not usurp management attention to the approval and attainment of plans.

The foregoing outline of a process, intended as a suggestion, is obviously designed for an organization of some size and complexity, a participative and collegial style of management, confronted with strategic issues of great difficulty. A variant of this process can readily be downsized to simpler organizations and less complicated problems. The essential elements in any case are (1) participation by key individuals in the identification of problems and strategic opportunities, (2) inclusion of personal preferences, organization values, and corporate capability in the analysis, (3) the marshaling of accurate and relevant data on further market growth, and (4) the recognition of financial constraints with respect to capital sources and projected return.

We return full circle to the proposition that redirection of strategy, always a problem in an ongoing company, consists, like the original conceptualization, of a reconciliation of market opportunity, corporate resources and capability, personal preferences, values, and ethical standards. The outcome determines the mission and character of a company with a set of identifying obligations to a number of constituencies. Commitment to strategy is essential to superior performance. That is a simple reason for the involvement of whatever number of people is required to make a success of whatever is intended. Strategic management in a small company need not be as cumbersome as in a large diversified corporation, but it has the same imperatives.

Getting people who know the business to identify issues needing resolution, communicating these issues to all the managers affected, and programming action leading to resolution usually lead to the articulation of a strategy to which annual operating plans—otherwise merely numerical extrapolations of hope applied to past experience—can be successively related. It is not our purpose here, however, to present a master design for formal planning systems. This is a specialty of its own, which, like all other such specialties, needs to be related to corporate strategy but not allowed to smother or substitute for it.

When formal plans are prepared and submitted as the program to which performance is compared as a basis for evaluation, managers in intermediate position are necessarily involved in initiating projects within a concept of strategy rather than proceeding ad hoc from situation to situation. Senior managers can be guided in their approval of investment decisions by a pattern more rational than their hunches, their instinct for risk, and their faith in the track record of those making proposals, important as all these are. They have a key question to ask: what impact upon present and projected strategy will this decision make?

Sustaining the strategic process requires monitoring resource allocation with awareness of its strategic—as well as operational—consequences and its social, political, and financial characteristics. Seeing to it that the process works right means that the roles of the middle-level general manager be known and appropriately supported.

Middle-level general managers occupy a role quite different from that of the senior general manager, relevant as is their experience as preparation for later advancement. With strategic language and summary corporate goals coming to them from their superiors and the language and problems of everyday operations coming to them from their subordinates, middle-level general managers have the responsibility of translating the operational proposals, improvisations, and piecemeal solutions of their subordinates into the strategic pattern suggested to them by their superiors.

Faced with the need to make reconciliation between short-term and long-term considerations, they must examine proposals and supervise operations with an eye to their effect on long-term development. As they transform general strategic directions into operating plans and programs, they are required to practice the overview of the general manager. Their responsibility for balanced attention to short- and long-term needs and for bringing diverse everyday activities within the stream of evolving strategy far outruns their authority either to require change in strategy or to alter radically the product line of their division.

General managers at middle level, certainly in a crucial position to implement strategy in such a way as to advance it rather than depart from it, need to be protected from such distractions as performance evaluation systems overemphasizing short-term performance and to be supported continually in their duty of securing results that run beyond their authority to order certain outcomes. They need to learn how to interpret the signals they get as proposals they submit for top-management approval are accepted or turned down. Their superiors will be dependent upon their judgment as their proposals for new investment come in. Their superiors will often also be guided more by past performance or the desire to assign greater responsibility than by the detailed content of their proposals. Their seniors will do well then to realize the complexity of their juniors' position and the necessity of their being equal to the exigencies of making tactical reality subject to strategic guidance and to directing observation of operations toward appropriate amendment of strategy.

Developing the accuracy of strategic decision in a multiproduct, technically complex company requires ultimately direct attention to organization climate and individual development. The judgment required is to conduct operations against a demanding operating plan and to plan simultaneously for a changing future, to negotiate with superiors and subordinates the level of expected performance, and to see, in short, the strategic implications of what is happening in the company and in its environment. The capacity of the general manager, outlined early in this book, must as part of the process of managing the strategy process be consciously cultivated if the firm is to mature in its capacity to conduct its business and in the ability to recognize in time the changes in strategy it must effect.

Executive development, viewed from the perspective of the general manager, is essentially the nurturing of the generalist capabilities referred to throughout this book. The management of the process of strategic decision must be concerned principally with continuous surveillance of the environment and development of the internal capabilities and distinctive competence of the company. The breadth of vision and the quality of judgment brought to the application of corporate capability to environmental opportunity are crucial. The senior managers who keep their organization involved continuously in appraising its performance against its goals, appraising its goals against the company's concept of its place in its industry and in society, and debating openly and often the continued validity of its strategy will find corporate attention to strategic questions gradually proving effective in letting the organization know what it is, what its activities are about, where it is going, and why its existence and growth are worth the best contributions of its members.

The chief executive of a company has as his or her highest obligation the management of a continuous process of strategic decision in which a succession of corporate objectives of ever-increasing appropriateness provides the means of economic contribution, the necessary commensurate return, and the opportunity for the men and women of the organization to live and develop through productive and rewarding careers.

The Strategic Function of the Board of Directors

If the first function of the chief executive is the management of the future-oriented purposeful development of the enterprise, then it is necessarily the responsibility of the board of directors to see that this job is adequately done. Although in the common conception of corporate governance the board is ultimately responsible, its outside directors cannot themselves customarily originate the strategy they must approve. The chief recourse of directors ratifying strategy in highly complex situations is not to substitute their judgment for that of management but to see that the proposals presented to them have been properly prepared and can be defended as strategically consistent and superior to available alternatives. If the proposals are flawed, they are usually withdrawn for revision by management. Although the board is usually unable to originate strategy, its detachment from operations equips it to analyze developing strategic decisions with fresh objectivity and breadth of experience. It can be free of the management myopia sometimes produced by operations in places where keeping things going obscures the direction they are taking.

Under pressure from the public, from the Securities and Exchange Commission, and indirectly from congressional committees, the board of directors for some years has been undergoing revitalization as the only available source of legitimacy for corporate power and assurance of corporate responsibility, given the archaism of corporation law and the dispersed ownership of the large public corporation.

The consensus developing in the current revival of board effectiveness is that working boards not only will actively support, advise, and assist management but also will monitor and evaluate management's performance in the attainment of planned objectives. Boards now are expected to exhibit in decision behavior their responsibility (while representing the economic interest of the shareholders) for the legality, integrity, and ethical quality of the corporation's activities and financial reporting, and their sensitivity to the interests of segments of society legitimately concerned about corporate performance.

For our purposes, the central function of a working board is to review the management's formulation and implementation of strategy and to exercise final authority in ratifying with good reason management's adherence to established objectives and policy or in contributing constructively to management's recommendation for change.

It is now widely recognized that boards should be diversely composed, should consist largely of outside directors, and should structure themselves to make their monitoring functions practicable. All firms registered on the New York Stock Exchange must have audit committees, for example, as a condition of membership. Their functions are to recommend to the board and then to shareholders the choice of external auditors, to ensure to the extent possible that the company's control personnel are generating and reporting accurate and complete data fairly representing the financial performance of the company, and to ascertain that internal auditors are examining in detail situations in which the company is vulnerable to fraud or improper behavior.

Despite the assumptions of some regulatory agency personnel, it is not possible for outside directors to detect fraud or identify questionable payments with their own eyes when well-intentioned and competent management auditors have not been able to do so. Their contribution is to inquire into the quality of intention, competence, and process, to observe the capability and command of information of those reporting to the committee, and to raise questions prompted by experience not available in the company. When necessary they recommend to the board replacement of controllers or change of auditors.

Executive compensation committees are expected to oversee the incentive and salary programs of the companies and to set the compensation of the most senior managers, in the course of that activity evaluating their performance. A trend is developing toward establishment of nominating committees to consider executive succession, board composition, and performance, and to recommend new members to the board. The flow of information to these committees is supposed to economize the time and improve the judgment of the independent directors and to enable them to appraise the caliber of the company's management. The possibility of overwhelming outsiders with information is always imminent. Information usable by the board cannot usually be siphoned out of the management information systems. Organization and selection to serve the special functions of the board are required.

In view of the difficulty entailed in enabling independent directors to pass judgment on strategic decisions, it is interesting to note that among the development of other committees (like public responsibility and legal affairs), strategy committees of the board, or whatever they might be called, are coming into wider use. It appears likely that as boards become aware of the need to relate approval of specific investment decisions to the purposes of the company, they may wish to focus the attention of some of the directors upon strategic questions now presented without prior detailed consideration to the full board.

The description I presented earlier of how strategic redirection is approached in some companies involves the participation of the board in management discussions of strategy before formal submission of recommendations to the board. This participation is indispensable to better understanding by outside directors of central strategic issues and to better knowledge of the capability of potential successors to the current CEO. It requires not only the capacity to separate board and management responsibilities and a scrupulous observance of the distinction but also the time to attend long discussions. A strategy committee would thus economize, as other committees do, board time and focus special experience and capability upon a set of related problems.

Like members of the audit and compensation committees, board members assigned to give additional time to the evaluation of total strategy would become familiar not necessarily with the detailed debates shaping specific strategic alternatives but with how the strategic process is managed in the company. You may wish to consider the extent to which familiarity with the strategy of your company and the ability to relate financial performance to it would affect the board's evaluation of the chief executive officer's performance and to what extent such familiarity is available otherwise.

In most boards at present it is assumed that the independent directors will support the chief executive until it is necessary to remove him. Removal ordinarily comes late after disaster has struck or after early strategic mistakes have produced repeated irretrievable losses. The go/no-go dilemma, which does not apply in any other superior-subordinate relationship in the corporation, could be replaced by discussion and debate at board level of strategic questions presented to the board by the chief executive officer. When interim remediable dissatisfaction with the quality of this discussion appeared, advice to the chief executive officer could be offered in time for it to do some good. Chief executives' longevity is extended in some situations by their securing the participation of the board in crucial strategic decisions. When one of these decisions fails after such participation, responsibility is shared by the board and the chief executive rather than borne by the latter alone. Routine ratification, without real discussion, does not secure the commitment of directors to any major decision. The attainment of board commitment is sometimes complicated by insecurity, unwillingness to share power, and lack of skill in board management on the part of the chief executive officers.

The problem of securing competent outside director preparation and participation is compounded by the relationship resulting from the simple fact that independent directors have ordinarily owed their board membership to the chairman or chief executive officer they are supposed to evaluate. The active participation of nominating committees has increased the independence of boards, especially when the chief executive officers participating in the selection process have wanted such a result.

The management of effective boards of directors has not been extensively studied. The power of strategy as a simplifying concept enabling independent directors to *know* the business (in a sense) without being *in* the business will one day be more widely tested at board level. If strategic management can be made less intuitive and more explicit, it will be possible for management directors and chief executive officers to identify existing strategy, evaluate it against the criteria we suggested at the beginning of this book, consider alternatives for improvement in the presence of the board, and make recommendations to a board equipped to make an intelligent critical response in strategic terms—that is, relating specific proposals to corporate strategy. The ability to sense the pattern of progress in the welter of operations is essential to all executives and directors who do not want to get lost in the trees around them.

Strategic management comes to its culmination in the chairmanship of effective boards. For the moment, the Securities and Exchange Commission, the Department of Justice, and the Federal Trade Commission appear to prefer the restructured and revitalized board of directors as the route to a kind of corporate governance sufficiently responsible to meet current concerns about autonomous management power. Most defenders of our mixed economic system prefer this approach to the introduction of new regulation. Voluntary adaptation to public expectations allows the special circumstances of each industry and company situation to be taken into account: regulation does not. On the other hand doing nothing unfortunately remains the easiest response to the call for voluntary action.

The mastery of the concept of strategy makes easier the kind of discussion in boardrooms that helps managements make better decisions. It performs this function by reducing the world of detail to be considered to those central aspects of external environment and internal resources that affect the company and bear on the definition of its business. The special skill involved in perceiving and communicating the strategic significance of a business decision may be of the highest importance in engaging independent directors in the exercise of their assumed responsibility and in establishing active and effective boards as normal adjuncts to competent professional management. Such a development may reduce the likelihood that corporate governance will be judged sufficiently irresponsible that radical legislative checks are imposed upon corporate freedom and initiative.

Index

A

Acoustic Research, Inc., 56–57
Aguilar, Frank J., 40
American Motors Corp., 22, 54

B

Bank of Boston, 66
Berg, Norman A., 26, 44
Boards of directors, 6, 74, 123–27
Bower, Joseph L., v, 44, 72 n
Business Policy; *see* Strategic management
  definition, viii
Business strategy, xi, 13

C

Carter, Jimmy, 5
Case, J. I., Co., 54
Christensen, C. Roland, v
Chrysler Corporation, 22
Compensation; *see* Executive compensation
Control systems, 105–9
  formal and informal controls, 106–7
Coordination, 88–89
Corporate competence, 45–49
Corporate conscience; *see* Social responsibility
Corporate governance, 123–27

Corporate resources; *see* Corporate competence
Corporate strategy
  commitment, 81–85, 91–95
  consistency, 28–29
  criteria for evaluation of, 27–31
  definition, 13–17
  diagrammed summary of, 21
  example of, 16
  formulation of, 18–20
    corporate competence and resources, 45–49
    opportunity and risk, 41–43
    personal values, 53–63
    social responsibility, 65–79
  formulation and implementation as major aspects of, 18
  functions and value of, 92–96
  implementation of, 20
    effective leadership, 5–9
    neglect of implementation, 82–84
    organization process and behavior, 97–112
    structure, coordination and information systems, 88–91
  interdependence of formulation and implementation, 85–88, 113–15
  kinds of strategies, 22–24
  matching opportunity and resources, 45–46

Corporate strategy—*Cont.*
opportunity, relationship to, 43–44
origin of concept, ix
problems of evaluation, 31–34
process aspects, 36, 62, 113–23
reasons for not articulating, 17–18
reconciling divergent categories of,
77–79
relation to corporate governance,
113–27
relation to environment, 35–51
relation to personal values, 53–63
relation to social responsibility,
65–79
terms in which defined, 16
twelve aspects of, 87–88
uniqueness of, 27–28, 49–51

D

Department of Justice, 126
Directors, boards of; *see* Boards of
directors
Distinctive competence; *see* Corporate
competence
Diversification, 23–27
DuPont, 59–61

E

Economic strategy, 18, 50
Emerson, Ralph Waldo, 28
Environmental opportunity
concepts for analysis of, 35–45
determinant of strategy, 43–45
identification of, 35–43
major trends, 36–39
nature of the company's
environment, 35–39
relation to competence, 45–47
surveillance of environment, 39–41
Ethical behavior
enforcing ethical standards, 107–9
moral component of strategy, 69–70
Evaluation of performance, 101–2
fallacy of single criterion, 98–101
need for multiple criteria, 100–101
Executive compensation, 102–5
Exxon Corporation, 67

F

Farwell, Frank, 54
Federal Trade Commission, 126
Ford, Henry, 22

Ford Motor Co., 22
Formulation of strategy; *see* corporate
strategy
Friedman, Milton, 70
Functional strategy, xi

G

General Dynamics Corporation, 66
General Electric Co., ix–x, 20, 25–26
General management
complexity of, 2–3
definition, 2–3
need for a theory of, 9–11
General managers; *see* also General
management
definition, 1
functions and skills of, 2–11
importance of in world of specialists,
89
primary function of, 7–8
General Motors Corp., 22, 28, 54, 60,
74, 84
Generalist; *see* General managers and
General management
Goals; *see* Corporate strategy
Goodpaster, Kenneth, E., 70n
Goodyear Tire and Rubber Co., 42
Gulf Oil Corp., 65

H

Hamermesh, Richard G., v
Hamm's Brewery, 16–17
Head, Howard, 58
Heublein, Inc., 16–17
Hewlett-Packard, 84
Hofer, Charles W., 44n
Hoffman, Abraham, 56–57
Hutton, E. F., 67

I

Implementation of strategy; *see*
Corporate strategy
Incrementalism, 17, 83–84
Innovative Corporation, the, 85–86,
97–98
Internal Revenue Service, 66
International Business Machines, Inc.,
20, 48, 84

J

Japanese Competition, vi–vii
Johns-Manville Corporation, 66
Johnson, Lyndon B., 5

K

Kennedy, John F., 5
Kets de Vries, Manfred, 62 n

L

Leadership
  general manager
    as architect of strategy, 7–9
    as organizational leader, 3–5
    as personal leader, 5–7
  quality of, 10–11
Learned, Edmund P., 55 n
Levitt, Theodore, 48 n
Lincoln Electric, 59
Lockheed Aircraft Corp., 65
Lodge, George, 38
Lorsch, Jay W., 59 n

M

Management, definition, 1; *see also*
  General management
Management development, 109–12,
  122
  importance of recruitment, 110
  relation to strategy, 111–12
  role of formal training, 110
Managers; *see* General managers
Matthews, John B., 70 n
Measurement; *see* Performance
  measurement
Mills, D. Quinn, 86 n
Motivation, 102–5
  executive compensation, 102–5

N

Nash, Laura L., 70 n
New York Stock Exchange, 124
New York Times, 14
NIKE Corporation, 98
Nixon, Richard, 5

O

Objectives; *see* Corporate strategy
Olivetti, Adriano, 54
Opportunity; *see* Environmental
  opportunity
Organizational processes
  control systems, 105–9
  establishment of standards, 99–101
  evaluation, 101–2
  fallacy of single criterion, 99–101
  individual development, 109–12

Organizational processes—*Cont.*
  measurement; *see* Performance
    measurement
  motivation, 102–5
  need for multiple criteria, 100–101
  recruitment and development,
    109–12
Organization structure
  relation of structure to strategy, 86,
    88–91
  responsibility, 119–21

P

Pattern in strategic decision, 13–15
Performance measurement, 99–105
Personal values
  awareness of, 61–63
  conflict among, 57–59
  definition, 59–60
  modification of, 59–61
  reconciling with economic strategy,
    54–57, 62–63
  relation to corporate strategy, 53–57
Pitts, Robert A., 44 n
Porter, Michael, v, 38
Prahalad, C. K., 44
Purpose; *see* Corporate strategy

Q–R

Quinn, James Brian, 83 n, 84 n, 90 n
Radio Corporation of America, 20
Resources; *see* Corporate resources
Responsibility; *see* Social responsibility
Responsibility to shareholders, 68
Reynolds, R. J., 16
Risk, identification of, 41–43
Romney, George, 54
Rumelt, Richard P., 25

S

Salter, Malcolm S., 25 n, 143 n
Schendel, Dan E., 44 n
Scott, Bruce R., 24, 43
Securities and Exchange Commission,
  65, 66, 123, 126
Shapiro, Irving S., 39 n
Simon, Herbert, 95
Smith, Adam, 68
Social responsibility
  case against involvement, 70
  case for involvement, 70–71

Social responsibility—*Cont.*
  categories of concern, 71–75
  American society, 72
  the firm, 73, 75–76
  the industry, 73
  local community, 72–73
  world society, 71–72
  component of strategy, 69–77
  conflict with control systems, 74
  resolution of conflicting
    responsibility, 77
Stages of corporate development,
  24–26, 43–44
Stevenson, Howard H., 45–46
Strategic management, viii, ix, xii
Strategy as process, 113–28

Strategy, corporate; *see* Corporate
  strategy
Strategy, economic; *see* Economic
  strategy

T–Z

Technological change, 36–37
Teledyne, Inc., 57
Underwood Corp., 20, 54
Values, personal; *see* Personal values
Villchur, Edgar, 56–57
Walton, Richard E., 91 n
Westinghouse Electric Corp., 25
Wrigley, Leonard, 25
Xerox Corporation, 20, 84
Zaleznik, Abraham, 62

This book has been set on a Quadex/Compu-graphic 8400 phototypsetting system, in 10 and 8 point Century Schoolbook, leaded 2 points. Chapter numbers are 24 point Helvetica Regular and Chapter titles are 20 point Helvetica Bold Italic. The size of the type page is 27 by 47 picas.